Striving against Satan

Striving against Satan

Joel Beeke

BRYNTIRION PRESS

ISBN 1 85049 219 0

Cover design: Evangelical Press

All Scripture quotations are from
the Authorised (King James) version.

Published by Bryntirion Press
Bryntirion, Bridgend CF31 4DX, Wales, UK
Printed by Gomer Press, Llandysul, Ceredigion SA44 4JL

With heartfelt appreciation to
my faithful colleague,
spiritual friend, and *gabba*,

Martin Holdt

Contents

Part Four
Knowing Satan's Defeat
in Our Personal Lives, Churches, and Nations

Preface

In his book, *Power Encounters*, David Powlison, editor of the *Journal of Biblical Counseling* and lecturer in practical theology at Westminster Theological Seminary, rightly argues that we urgently need to fight Satan by reclaiming biblical, traditional, spiritual warfare as set forth by Paul in Ephesians 6:10-20. We live in a society that has become increasingly pagan and has brought itself into a pervasive array and bondage of addictions. Troubled or bizarre behaviour has become commonplace; many people are experiencing a heightened sense of the presence of evil. Missionaries and anthropologists alert us to animistic cultures and demon possessions. Satanism is flourishing in Western nations. Since the 1970s, numbers of charismatics, dispensationalists, and theologians of the so-called 'third wave of the Holy Spirit' have been teaching and practising various forms of 'deliverance ministries' to cast out inhabiting demons. Frank Peretti's books have only added to the confusion, influencing thousands to see demons lurking everywhere.

On the other hand, millions in modern civilisation don't believe the devil exists, or at least have exorcised him from their working vocabulary, even though the devil is a primary explanation for the plight of modern civilisation. This attitude has even permeated the church. The nineteenth-century preacher, Charles Spurgeon, could already say in his day, 'Certain theologians, nowadays, do not believe in the existence of Satan. It is singular when children do not believe in the existence of their own father.'

Biblical, clear-headed thinking about Satan and spiritual warfare is sorely needed today. Particularly as believers we need to be cognizant that the battle against Satan and his forces of evil is fierce, spiritual, and necessary. We must know our adversary. We must know Satan's personality and history. We must know his strategies, his power, and his weaknesses. We must know how to withstand him and what spiritual weapons to take up against him. We must defeat him by faith, through lives that bear fruit and spread the truth.

This book addresses this need from a practical perspective. Its chapters enlarge upon five addresses given at the Metropolitan Tabernacle School of Theology in London on July 6-8, 2004. The first address (chapters 1-6), examines the personality and history of Satan. The second address (chapters 7-8), shows how believers are to exploit Satan's weaknesses by fighting defensively and offensively. The third address (chapters 9-10), relying heavily on old classics, exposes Satan's devices and expounds our remedies for them. The concluding addresses examine how we can defeat Satan in our personal lives and in our churches and nations (chapters 11-13).

I again wish to thank Dr Peter and Jill Masters for their hospitality and friendship, and for repeatedly inviting me to serve the historic Metropolitan Tabernacle. Thanks, too, to the helpful staff at the Tabernacle. What a joy it is to speak and fellowship at the Met Tab School of Theology! Hearty thanks to my dear wife Mary, to my children (Calvin, Esther, and Lydia), and to the Heritage Netherlands Reformed Congregation and the Puritan Reformed Theological Seminary for granting me the time to absent myself from my regular round of duties to serve at the Tabernacle.

May God graciously use this book to teach us all how to be more aware of Satan and his devices, and how to wage a more successful battle against him.

Part One
Knowing the Enemy:
The Personality and History of Satan

Chapter 1

A Holy War

If you are a true believer, Satan hates you. He hates you because you bear the image of Christ, because you are the peculiar workmanship of God created in Christ Jesus unto good works, and because you were snatched from his power.

You deserted Satan, and you fled his territory. By grace, you acknowledged Christ as your Lord and Master. You testify with Peter, 'Thou art the Christ, the Son of the living God' (Matt. 16:16). Satan hates you because Christ is within you and because you love Christ.

Satan wants you back. As Jesus said to his disciples, 'Behold, Satan hath desired to have you, that he may sift you as wheat' (Luke 22:31), so Satan wants to sift you like wheat. Do not overestimate or underestimate Satan. He is not a fallen deity; he is not God. He is only a fallen angel. He is not almighty. Yet Satan is a powerful enemy. John Blanchard writes, 'We are opposed by a living, intelligent, resourceful and cunning enemy who can outlive the oldest Christian, outwork the busiest, outfight the strongest and outwit the wisest.'

Every true believer is engaged in what the Bible describes as spiritual warfare (Gen. 3:15; Rev. 12:7). John Bunyan called it a holy war. This spiritual warfare or holy war involves a perpetual battle against three great enemies: the devil, the world, and the flesh.

A fierce battle
The battle against Satan and the devils is *fierce*. Life and death are at stake, involving forces of light and darkness. Dark principalities and powers are under Satan's dominion and subject to his

orders. Satan's lieutenants are devils who delight to carry out his orders. Satan's army is aggressive, malignant, and cruel, and its power is in high places above us and around us. This army is too powerful for us to fight in our own strength, yet we cannot compromise with Satan or surrender to him. Rather, we must resist the devil (James 4:7) by conscientiously following the Bible's directions for victory over Satan.

A spiritual battle

The battle against Satan and his devils is *spiritual*. We do not fight this enemy with guns, tanks, or atomic weapons. Nor do we fight merely against flesh and blood. As Paul wrote to the Ephesians, 'We wrestle not against flesh and blood, but against principalities, against powers, against the rulers of the darkness of this world, against spiritual wickedness in high places' (Eph. 6:12). This battle is not for worldly power, possessions, or honour, Paul says. It aims higher, at the spiritual realities of truth, righteousness, and the glory of the living God and his Son. Behind our visible enemies of flesh and blood is an army of spiritual, invisible adversaries. Spiritual warfare is a battle against invisible enemies with invisible weapons who oppose the cause and kingdom of Jesus Christ.

We wrestle against Satan's invisible, innumerable, powerful army. Wrestling is close, spiritual conflict. It is intense and strenuous. In wrestling, opponents do not maintain distance from each other; they seize each other. Whether as the prince of darkness or as an angel of light, Satan engages us hand-to-hand and foot-to-foot in life and death spiritual warfare.

A necessary battle

The battle against Satan and his devils is *necessary*. Much as our world today cannot escape the war against terrorism, so we cannot escape war with Satan. Like it or not, we are at war. We cannot plead pacifism or medical deferment, nor can we avoid the bullets and the bombs. To be in the midst of war, and not realize it, is most dangerous. If we ignore the enemy, we set ourselves up for defeat. Paul commands us to 'put on the whole armour of

God, that ye may be able to stand against the wiles of the devil' (Eph. 6:11).

Too many Christians today pay little attention to Paul's command. Too many churches speak more about disarmament than armament. And too many preachers promote a broadly ecumenical 'universal brotherhood' that embraces a variety of religions rather than expose the antithesis between two opposing kingdoms in this world.

As unpleasant as the subject of Satan is, we need to study it. The Puritan Thomas Brooks wrote: 'Christ, the Scripture, your own hearts, and Satan's devices, are the four prime things that should be first and most studied and searched' (*Precious Remedies,* p. 15). If we have poorly formed ideas about Satan's goals, strengths, and limitations, we become careless. We underestimate the power of our enemy.

In this short book, we will study Satan and his devices. I trust that what we learn will assist us to fight strenuously, to fight well, and to fight on, until we obtain complete victory over the enemy (cf. Heidelberg Catechism, Q. 127). May God help us in the battle.

Chapter 2

Satan in the Old Testament

S atan's personality and history are the foundation of the doctrine of Satan, which is sometimes called satanology or, when extended to Satan's fallen angelic helpers, demonology. The career of Satan, which extends from before man's creation (Job 38:7) to eternity future, forms a significant doctrine in the Scriptures.

The Bible is so full of references to Satan that it would seem impossible to hold to the Christian faith without accepting the devil's reality. His existence is attested in nine Old Testament books (Genesis, Leviticus, Deuteronomy, 1 Chronicles, Job, Psalms, Isaiah, Ezekiel, and Zechariah) and by every New Testament writer.

Satan's name and origin

Satan is a Hebrew word that means 'an accuser or adversary, one who resists'. The term is used nineteen times in the Old Testament, fourteen of which are in Job 1 and 2. *Satan* is also mentioned in 1 Chronicles 21:1, Psalm 109:6, and Zechariah 3:1–2.

Scholars have long disputed whether the term *Satan* is a proper name or a title. In Job and Zechariah, the definite article precedes the noun for Satan, so that its literal translation is 'the Satan' or 'the accuser'. However, 1 Chronicles 21:1 and Psalm 109:6 do not include the definite article before 'Satan'. Some scholars have concluded from this that the term *Satan* should be regarded as a title in Job and Zechariah and as a proper name in 1 Chronicles and Psalm 109 (Elwell, ed., *Evangelical Dictionary of Biblical Theology,* p. 714).

Satan and all the other angels were created by God as spirit beings (Ps. 148:2,5; Heb. 1:7,14). Job 1 indicates that Satan was once probably one of the highest and brightest angels of God, who had a special place of prominence in his service to God. Ezekiel 28:12-15 tells us what Satan was like before he sinned. Though speaking to the king of Tyre, the prophet Ezekiel was speaking beyond the king to Satan himself. He describes Satan as 'the anointed cherub that covereth' (v. 14), 'full of wisdom, and perfect in beauty' (v. 12), and morally blameless (v. 15). He was in 'Eden the garden of God' (v. 13), placed 'upon the holy mountain of God' (v. 14).

Donald Grey Barnhouse writes, 'Satan awoke in the first moment of his existence in the full-orbed beauty and power of his exalted position, surrounded by all the magnificence which God gave him. He saw himself as above all the hosts in power, wisdom, and beauty. Only at the throne of God itself did he see more than he himself possessed.' Barnhouse concludes that Satan, before his fall, 'occupied the role of prime minister for God, ruling possibly over the universe but certainly over this world' (*Invisible War,* pp. 26-27).

Satan's fall and activity in Paradise

Ezekiel 28:15-19 goes on to tell us that Satan fell from his high position because of his preoccupation with his own beauty and glory and because of his foolish ambition to unseat the God of glory. Satan's sin originated in pride, grew into self-deception, and ended in rebellious ambition. That rebellion led him to induce a large number of angels to join him in opposing God (Rev. 12:4). God then threw Satan and all the rebellious angels out of heaven to the earth (Ezek. 28:16-17). Satan lost for ever his original position as the anointed cherub of God (Jude 6).

Since Satan could no longer attack God directly in heaven, he marshalled his evil efforts against man, the crown of God's creation. Satan's activity in history is first recorded in Genesis 3. We are told that Satan came as a serpent into Paradise, where he approached Eve. Satan used several techniques on Eve that he still uses on us today:

1. *Satan put God's command in a negative light.* He asked Eve, 'Yea, hath God said, Ye shall not eat of every tree of the garden?' (Gen. 3:1b). God had actually stated that Adam and Eve could eat from all the thousands of trees in the Garden of Eden except one. Eve corrected Satan, saying, 'We may eat of the fruit of the trees of the garden: but of the fruit of the tree which is in the midst of the garden, God hath said, Ye shall not eat of it, neither shall ye touch it, lest ye die' (Gen. 3:2-3).

2. *Satan impugned God's motive and character.* He told Eve, 'Ye shall not surely die: for God doth know that in the day ye eat thereof, then your eyes shall be opened, and ye shall be as gods' (Gen. 3:4-5). Satan sought to impugn God's character by persuading Eve to question God's goodness. God was not good and fair, he suggested, since he had restricted their freedom and forbidden eating from the tree of the knowledge of good and evil.

3. *Satan said that man could be like God.* Satan sought to transfer his own goal to the human race when he told Eve, 'And ye shall be as gods, knowing good and evil' (Gen. 3:5b). In other words, Adam and Eve could decide for themselves what was right and wrong. They could decide what they wanted to do. They did not have to listen to others, not even God. They could be their own gods. But that was a half-truth because they would know good and evil, but they could never be as God. Nor did Satan explain that without divine grace they would not have the power to do good or to avoid evil.

4. *Satan made sin look good.* Genesis 3:6 tells us, 'And when the woman saw that the tree was good for food, and that it was pleasant to the eye, and a tree to be desired to make one

wise, she took of the fruit thereof, and did eat, and gave also unto her husband with her; and he did eat.'

Satan under God's control, despite his ongoing attacks

Despite Satan's success in getting Adam and Eve to disobey God, to break covenant with God, and to plunge the entire human race into sin, Satan remained under the control of God throughout the entire Old Testament era. That is evident from Satan's relation to Saul in 1 Samuel 16:14–23 and in Satan's dealings with God and Job in Job 1. Satan could not act beyond the limits fixed by God in his sovereign power as the Creator. Without God's permissive will, he 'cannot so much as move' (cf. Heidelberg Catechism, Q. 28). That's what Martin Luther meant when he said, 'Even the devil is God's devil.'

Nonetheless, Satan has regularly bruised the heel of the woman's seed since Eden. The nations walked in his darkness, in blind unbelief, and in a host of sins. But God sovereignly chose a people for himself in the midst of Satan's rule of darkness. Even within his chosen people of Israel, however, darkness often prevailed. Yet God kept his 7,000 who refused to bow the knee to Baal (1 Kings 19:18). And he promised his remnant that walked by faith and challenged the dominion of sin, that he would soon send the Deliverer from sin and death.

Satan's influence is evident in the conflict between Cain and Abel, Ishmael and Isaac, Esau and Jacob, Egypt and Israel. Satan's goal is always the same: to wipe out the chosen seed. Witness the command of Pharaoh to destroy all of Israel's male children. Witness Egypt's attack on the Israelites at the Red Sea. Witness Haman's plot against Esther and her people.

Satan lurks at every turn throughout the Old Testament, trying to overthrow the long-term purposes of God. Satan incited David to number the people (1 Chron. 21:1). Satan accused Joshua the high priest of sin (Zech. 3:1). Satan tried to impoverish God's chosen people through heathen practices associated with orgiastic rites (1 Kings 18:28), witchcraft (2 Kings 9:22), occultism (2 Kings 21:6-7), and soothsaying (Micah 5:12). But Satan's evil campaigns, no matter how well planned, continually fail, for God uses them to fulfil rather than to thwart his purposes. Satan questioned Job's piety by saying it was based on self-interest, but in the end, God refined his servant Job through fiery trials and brought him forth as gold. Satan planned to get Balaam to curse Israel, but the Spirit of God came upon Balaam so that he prophesied instead about God's gracious will for Israel. Satan is so ruled by God's bidding, Calvin said, 'as to be compelled to render him service' (*Institutes,* 1.14.17).

What a comfort it is to know that our greatest enemy's evil schemes are fully under the control of our best Friend, so that 'we know that all things work together for good to them that love God, to them who are the called according to his purpose' (Rom. 8:28). That's why Calvin could conclude, 'Even the devil can sometimes act as a doctor for us.'

Chapter 3

Satan in the New Testament

The doctrine of Satan developed further during the centuries between the testaments and in the New Testament. Intertestamental literature refers to Satan as Belial, Mastema, and Sammael. Satan is described as chief of an army of demons that war against God and his angels. Satan tempts believers, attacks them, and leads devils and unregenerate people against God (Jubilees 11:5; 17:16; 1 Enoch 40:7).

The intertestamental literature attributes evil in Old Testament times directly to Satan more often than the Old Testament does (Wis. Sol. 2:24). The Old Testament usually doesn't name Satan directly, but in the intertestamental writings Satan is explicitly described as 'a fallen angel' (1 Enoch 29:4), who is in charge of the 'fallen angels' spoken of in Genesis 6:1–4 (Jubilees 10:5–8; 19:28).

Satan's names

The New Testament most often refers to Satan as 'the devil' *(diabolos)*. That term, which means traducer or slanderer, is used sixty times in the New Testament [KJV], forty times in the Gospels alone. Satan is slanderer *par excellence.* He slanders God to man, as he did to Eve; he slanders, at times, man to God, as he did in Job's case; and he slanders man to man.

The term *Satan* occurs thirty-four times in the New Testament [KJV]. Half of those terms are in the Gospels and Acts, and half in the Epistles and Revelation. All but six of the references refer to 'the Satan'. Other New Testament names for Satan include the Accuser (Rev. 12:10), the Adversary (1 Pet. 5:8), Apollyon

(Rev. 9:11), Beelzebub (Matt. 12:24), Belial (2 Cor. 6:15), the Dragon (Rev. 12:7), God of this world (2 Cor. 4:4), Prince of the power of the air (Eph. 2:2), Prince of this world (John 12:31), the Serpent (Rev. 20:2), the Tempter (Matt. 4:3), and a roaring Lion (1 Pet. 5:8).

How diverse and powerful these names reveal Satan to be! One Puritan, Edward Reynolds, put it this way, 'Satan has three titles in the Scriptures, setting forth his malignity against the church of God: a dragon, to note his malice; a serpent, to note his subtlety; and a lion, to note his strength.'

Satan's personality, army, and subjects

These names teach us that Satan is not an impersonal evil force. He possesses all the traits of personality, such as intellect (2 Cor. 11:3), emotion (Rev. 12:17), and will (2 Tim. 2:26). Personal pronouns are also used of him (Matt. 4:1-12). Being a person, he is held morally accountable by the Lord (Matt. 25:41). That's why the New Testament speaks of him as proud, rebellious, lawless, and slanderous, and why he is called a liar, a deceiver, a distorter, and an imitator.

The New Testament reveals Satan as the ruler of a host of fallen angels (Matt. 25:41), and as the head of a well-organized army of spiritual agents. Terms such as principalities, powers, and rulers of the darkness of this world indicate ranks in Satan's army (Eph. 6:12). By means of these ranks of demons, Satan, like a competent general, gathers his information and carries out his programme throughout his worldwide kingdom of darkness.

Satan and his demons carry out their evil, devilish activity among people in the world who do not acknowledge Christ as Lord (Mark 4:15; John 8:44; Col. 1:13). With temptations ranging from asceticism to libertinism and from intellectual theism to crass occultism, he blinds their minds, seeks to prevent their believing in Christ alone for salvation, and strives to retain their allegiance to himself (2 Cor. 4:4; Luke 8:12). That's why his human followers are called 'the children of the wicked one' (Matt. 13:38), his 'ministers' (2 Cor. 11:15), and 'the children of the devil' (1 John 3:10).

Demon-possession

In some cases, Satan and his demons enter into and control their followers so fully that they engage in 'demon-possession'. Luke 8:30 describes a man whose name was called Legion because 'many devils were entered into him'. Particularly prior to Christ's death and resurrection, Satan and his demons were permitted to exert dreadful, powerful, overt attacks upon some people's minds and bodies. God permitted that power, in part, so that people might deeply know their need for a deliverer, and that the power of Christ to deliver them would be prominently displayed. Demon-possessions could produce blindness (Matt. 12:22), paralysis (Acts 8:7), convulsions (Luke 9:39), paroxysms (Mark 9:17, 20, 26), self-destruction (Mark 9:22), superhuman strength (Mark 5:4), personality splits (Mark 5:6-10), special knowledge to identify Jesus (Mark 5:7), or insanity and bizarre behaviour (Luke 8:27; Matt. 17:15). All of this shows that there is no kind of affliction, mental or physical, that Satan and his demons are unwilling to bring upon people. Common to all these is destructiveness, for Satan is ever the destroyer. The gospel authors are careful to differentiate demonic activity from various physical sicknesses (Matt. 4:24; Luke 4:40-41).

Satan is bitterly opposed to God and seeks to alienate everyone from God; hence Satan also wages intense war against the followers of Christ (Luke 8:33; 1 Cor. 7:5). Since every believer is indwelt by the Holy Spirit and belongs to Jesus, no believer can be demon-possessed (1 Cor. 6:19). John affirms this by saying that Jesus, who is in us, is greater than Satan who is in the world (1 John 4:4). Nevertheless, Satan still so influenced Peter's thinking that Jesus had to say firmly to Peter, 'Get thee behind me, Satan!' (Matt. 16:23). Luke 22:31 tells us that Satan wanted to sift all of the disciples as wheat to test them. Revelation 12:10 says that Satan seeks to accuse believers before God.

Satan versus Christ

The conflict between the devil and the Seed of the woman took the centre stage upon the incarnation of the word. The coming of Jesus Christ in the fullness of time was God's greatest move against Satan in spiritual warfare. Jesus spoke more about Satan and demons than anyone else in the Bible. Satan and his demons unleashed their strongest fury against Jesus, whose sinless humanity motivated Satan to tempt him in special ways. In the desert of Judea, Christ stepped from the water of baptism into the fire of temptation. For forty days, Satan attacked Jesus in the lusts of the flesh, the lusts of the eyes, and the boastful pride of life, trying to get Christ's sacred humanity under his control (Matt. 4:1-11). Satan tempted Jesus to independence (4:3-4), indulgence (4:5-7), and idolatry (4:8-10). He tempted Jesus to turn away from the will of his Father, from the word of God, and from the cross. His underlying goal was to make Christ's substitution unnecessary by offering Christ glory without the cross, just as he had promised glory to Eve without obedience to God.

Jesus held his ground, repeatedly driving away Satan and his demons from himself, and subsequently, from other people in his public ministry. He engaged in a ministry of proclaiming deliverance to the captives (Luke 4:18). In his confrontation with the Pharisees over the healing of a demon-possessed man who was blind and mute, Jesus made clear his intent to drive Satan out of people's lives (Matt. 12:26). Jesus also liberated a woman whom Satan had kept bound for eighteen years (Luke 13:16).

In Gethsemane, Satan unleashed all the powers of hell. He brought Jesus to his knees, crawling as a worm and dripping with such bloody sweat that God's Son cried out in agony, 'O my Father, if it be possible, let this cup pass from me' (Matt. 26:39). Oh, what bruisings of the soul Christ experienced at the hands of Satan's instrument, Judas Iscariot! No wonder he said to the satanic forces, 'This is your hour, and the power of darkness' (Luke 22:53).

The satanic attack continued at Gabbatha, where Christ was forced to wear a purple robe and a crown of thorns while he was scourged, mocked, slapped, and bruised. Finally, at Golgotha, Satan unleashed all the forces of evil once more. The bulls of Bashan encompass the suffering Messiah (Ps. 22:12). Every insult is heaped on Jesus; the brutal solders, the cruel spectators, and the selfish priests and elders in their holy robes of office engaged in satanic mocking while Christ hung on the cross in the naked flame of his Father's wrath, rejected by heaven and earth, and attacked by hellish powers. His unfathomable cry of agony rang through the dark realm of nature, 'My God, my God, why hast thou forsaken me?' (Matt. 27:46).

Luther once spent an entire morning trying to comprehend this agony, only to rise from his knees, confessing: 'God forsaken of God; who can comprehend it?' Indeed, that truth is incomprehensible. But this much we know: Satan was defeated on the cross, once and for all. Hebrews 2:14 says, 'Through death he [that is, Christ] might destroy him that had the power of death, that is, the devil.' Jesus spoke of the cross as a kind of cosmic exorcism in John 12:31-32, 'Now is the judgment of this world: now shall the prince of this world be cast out. And I, if I be lifted up from the earth, will draw all men unto me.' The victory belongs to Christ because of his perfect obedience throughout the most severe tests instigated by Satan.

Through his life, death, resurrection, and ascension, Christ single-handedly broke the power of the oppressor. Satan lost his suffocating rule over the nations. The balance of power was turned. In the Old Testament era, flashes of light appeared in the darkness. But now, in and through Christ, the light has dawned. Christ's abiding light and glory now outweigh Satan's remaining evil and darkness.

After Christ's resurrection and ascension into heaven, demon-possession greatly diminished. The book of Acts reports a few instances which generally emerged when the gospel was first brought to an area. Peter and Philip both cast out demons on at least one occasion (Acts 5:16; 8:7). Paul delivered a young woman from a fortune-telling demon at Philippi and cast out demons at Ephesus (16:16-18; 19:11-12). But the New Testament epistles—though speaking often of satanic opposition against the church (Rom. 8:38-39; 1 Cor. 2:8, 15:24-26; Eph. 1:20-22, 3:10, 6:12; Col. 1:16, 2:15)—make little mention of demon-possession and give no instructions for exorcism. Demon possession does not seem to have been a significant problem in the established New Testament church.

Satan versus the New Testament church

Satan, however, did not easily admit defeat. He continued to bruise the heel of Christ's church in other ways. The New Testament church found victory in Christ only through the same kind of suffering and bruising that the Saviour experienced. Acts tells us how Satan brought trouble into the church by persuading Ananias and Sapphira to disrupt the church's peace with a lie (Acts 5:3). Satan tempted Corinthian church members to abandon self-control in sexual matters (1 Cor. 7:5). Satan tempted Paul by inflicting on him 'a thorn in his flesh' (2 Cor. 12:7) and by preventing Paul from travelling to Thessalonica (1 Thess. 2:18). Satan persecuted believers in Smyrna (Rev. 2:9–10) and deceived the nations of the earth (Rev. 20:7–8), disguising himself as an angel of light to accomplish his purposes (2 Cor. 11:14). His demons serve as agents of apostasy (1 Tim. 4:1-3), and promoters of the Man of Lawlessness and the spirit of antichrist (2 Thess. 2:9; Rev. 2:18-29; 9:1-11).

Throughout all of Satan's opposition, the church pressed on. Despite temporary setbacks, the gates of hell did not prevail against her, for Jesus is mightier than Satan.

Chapter 4

Satan in Church History

The church's battle with Satan did not end with the Book of Revelation. Satan continued to work both within the church and from without. He sowed seeds of corruption, heresy, strife, and schism in the visible church. He instigated waves of persecution against the visible church across the centuries.

Satan presided over the rise of prelacy, as the clergy sought to enlarge their powers and domains as bishops, archbishops, patriarchs, and popes. Satan fostered the growth of superstition regarding the sacraments, including baptismal regeneration, transubstantiation, and the substitution of the mass in the place of the Lord's Supper. Satan encouraged the introduction of pagan practices into Christian worship, such as use of the vestments of the pagan Roman priesthood, or the worship of pictures, crucifixes, statues, and relics of the saints. Satan inspired many to embrace false teaching about the Trinity, the natures and person of Christ, or the canon of Holy Scripture, not to mention false ideas about the life to come, such as 'purgatory' and 'limbo'. The corruption of the visible church and the rise of the false church were, in significant measure, the work of Satan.

As the once-flourishing churches of the Middle East and North Africa became increasingly corrupt and weak, Satan launched a counter-attack, inspiring the visions and sayings of a false prophet, named Mohammad, rousing the tribes of Arabia to follow him as an army in a campaign to plant the religion of Islam across the map of the ancient world by force. The Christian church was crushed to the ground in many places. Today, after a long period of slumber, Islam, particularly in its radical elements, has been roused again by Satan to spread its darkness into new lands, and to foster a new reign of terror throughout the world.

Working through the civil authorities, Satan has launched waves of persecution against the church from ancient times through the Reformation, the Great Awakening, times of revival, and throughout the twentieth century, in which more Christians died for their faith than in all previous centuries combined. Noteworthy as the work of Satan are the rise of Hitler's 'National Socialism' in Germany, which targeted Jews and Christians for destruction, and the long reign of terror conducted against Christianity in Russia, Eastern Europe, and China by atheistic Marxism or 'International Socialism'. Yet, the times of severe persecution have often been the church's most blessed times. Tertullian rightly compared the church to a mowed field. 'The more frequently it is cut, the more it grows', Tertullian said. Church history confirms that the blood of the martyrs has been the seed of the church.

Views of Satan

Views of Satan have varied over the centuries. The Ancient and Medieval Church often developed excessive and somewhat fanciful views of Satan, and increasingly encouraged the office of exorcist. Origen, the church's first systematic theologian, said Lucifer (Isa. 14:12–15) was the Satan who had revolted and fallen from heaven because of pride, but was still offered mercy by God. Augustine agreed that Satan was Lucifer, but rejected Origen's fanciful idea that Satan could be reconciled with God. Augustine believed that demons incite people to crimes and wickedness, possess considerable knowledge, and are able to attack people. Thomas Aquinas believed that Satan was once the highest angel who, through pride, fell immediately after creation, seducing those who followed him to become his subjects.

Martin Luther attributed much to the devils, though he reacted to the excesses of the Medieval Church. He particularly spoke out against the office of exorcist, which had been established early on in the history of Christianity and reached a crescendo in the Late Middle Ages. Luther said that, unlike Christ and the apostles, 'we cannot of ourselves expel the evil spirits, nor must we even attempt it' (Leahy, *Satan Cast Out,* p. 113). Luther did believe, however, that demons infest 'woods, water, swamps, and deserted places', and that they are continually 'plotting against our life and welfare' (*Table Talk,* p. 172). Nevertheless, the word, believed on and prayed over, is sufficient to withstand Satan. 'The devil hates the word of God more than any other thing', Luther wrote (*Luther's Works,* comment on Psalm 94:6). In 'A Mighty Fortress is Our God', he wrote, 'We tremble not, we fear no ill; They shall not overpow'r us. This world's prince may still, Scowl fierce as he will, He can harm us none, He's judged; the deed is done; One little word can fell him' (*Lutheran Worship,* no. 298).

John Calvin refuted those 'who babble of devils as nothing else than evil emotions' by pointing to texts that prove the existence of Satan and the devils. He asserted that Scripture's teachings about Satan and his demons ought to arouse us 'to take precaution against their stratagems' (*Institutes,* 1.14.13–19), especially by outfitting ourselves with faith, prayer, and all the other pieces of the armour of God that Paul expounds in Ephesians 6:10-18. Like Luther, however, Calvin spoke out against the Roman Catholic excesses concerning demon activity; he avoided the superstitions of the day and yet viewed demon-possession as a present reality.

The Puritans particularly emphasised how Satan imitates the work of the Holy Spirit. Reflecting on the Great Awakening in the 1740s, Jonathan Edwards wrote, 'There are many false spirits, exceeding busy with men, who often transform themselves into angels of light, and do in many [remarkable] ways, with great subtlety and power, mimic the operations of the Spirit of God' (*Religious Affections,* p. 69).

Demon activity does not cohere with the modern worldview and so has been marginalized, or, in many cases, denied. Following the naturalism of the nineteenth and twentieth centuries, liberal and neo-orthodox Christianity rejected Satan's literal existence as primitive superstition. One such sceptic, Rudolf Bultmann, wrote, 'It is impossible to use electric light and to avail ourselves of modern medical and surgical discoveries, and at the same time to believe in the New Testament world of demons and spirits.' Today, science and technology underscore the dominating ideology that only the 'natural world' exists. 'Can a modern believe that God controls lightning and thunder if a meteorologist can use satellite pictures and computer modeling to predict the storm a week ahead of time?' asks David Powlison (*Power Encounters,* p. 23).

Even churchgoing people have exorcised the devil from their working vocabulary. According to a recent study, 76% of Anglicans deny the reality of Satan. Many theologians and psychologists have reinterpreted the biblical accounts of demon-possession to fit their own theological and psychological theories. Ironically, these denials of the biblical devil by churchmen and theologians have been accompanied by an explosion of new interest in witchcraft, astrology, paganism, and Satanism. Today covens of witches, frolicking bands of pagans, and congregations of 'the church of Satan' flourish in cities of Europe and North America. Some authors suggest that there are 500 identifiable satanic groups in the United States alone and 10,000 worldwide members. These numbers are hard to establish since most of these groups lack official headquarters and organisations, and do not publish their statistics. We do know, however, that Satanism is openly practised today as a legal religion in North America.

Modern Satanism was introduced into the United States by Aleister Crowley (b. 1875), who was reared in a godly home in England, where he was introduced to occult ideas and techniques by a well-known occultist, Eliphas Levi. Crowley's teaching that Satan was mightier than God, combined with his bizarre religious and sexual rituals often performed while under the influence of drugs, influenced another Englishman, Gerald Gardner. A self-proclaimed witch, Gardner's books helped establish rituals of modern witchcraft founded upon the Mother Goddess. Gardner, and later Anton LaVey (b. 1930), who founded the Church of Satan in 1966, popularised the image of Baphomet, the honoured god, as a symbol of witchcraft and Satanism. 'God is dead and Satan lives' has become a password for rituals in many of LaVey's local grottoes or 'congregations'. Since the 1970s, numerous groups have split off from LaVey's church and formed other satanic groups.

Situated between those who deny Satan and those who worship him, Pentecostals and charismatics have increasingly emphasized the reality of Satan and the importance of spiritual warfare. They often fall into the error of encouraging an unhealthy interest in devils. They find a demon behind every problem they face; personal responsibility gives way to demonic influence. Deeds of the flesh become demons to be exorcised. All of this promotes an increasingly popular occult spirituality. Superstitious remedies, such as spiritual mapping and exorcism rituals, become more popular than the scriptural response of confession of sin, repentance, and new obedience to Christ.

In the last few years many people have become more aware of Satan and his devils. Christian and secular bookstores are filled with books on angels and demons. Popular writers, like M. Scott Peck, are openly becoming converts to belief in the devil's reality. Today is an opportune time for word-centred evangelicals to promote a biblically balanced view of Satan and demons that avoids both denial and obsession.

Chapter 5

Satan Today

Since the death and resurrection of Christ, Satan has been bound. God's sentence upon Satan in Genesis 3:15 has been executed. Revelation 20 says that Satan can no more deceive the nations. That means he can no longer prevent the spread of the gospel among the nations. Satan has been chained by the death and resurrection of Jesus Christ. The great obstacle to the evangelisation of the nations—Satan's deceptive hold over the nations—has been removed.

But this doesn't mean that Satan has stopped working in today's world. God continues to allow Satan to work in the world for now. Demons still do Satan's bidding, as do unsaved people who are in Satan's service, and even, from time to time, God's people, when caught in Satan's sieve. Under the permissive decree of God, Satan rules unbelievers through the present evil world system (2 Cor. 4:3–4; Eph. 2:2; Col. 1:13).

Demon possession today

Occasional cases of demon possession continue to be reported by many missionaries, especially those who introduce the gospel into pagan territory. As people increasingly revert to pagan ideas and drift into the occult, we should not be surprised to hear of such cases in the future.

Frederick Leahy concludes that present-day demon possession may be voluntary or involuntary, permanent or spasmodic. Generally, one's personality is suppressed or a double personality emerges. In either case, the demon uses the victim as his instrument in ways that distinguish demon possession from mental insanity. Deliverance, when it comes, is usually sudden, and the one healed seems to have no recollection of what he said or did (*Satan Cast Out,* pp. 80, 90, 91).

There is a vast difference between the casting out of demons by Jesus and the apostles and present-day exorcism, which is rooted in pagan practices. Leahy writes, 'Pagan exorcisms are simply a trick by which Satan brings people increasingly under his power. The stronger demon in the sorcerer will most certainly expel the demon in a possessed person. But that person is not healed. He has not been delivered from the power of the enemy. The expelled demon can and probably will return' (p. 103).

Ministers and ordinary believers today should not try to be exorcists. Grave dangers are involved with dabbling in exorcism. One such danger is the potential of leading a person into unreality and psychosis. Dan VanderLugt writes, 'As fallen people, each of us has a deep, largely unconscious fear of seeing our sins as they really are. Even Christians who have grown in maturity for many years are quick to admit that they have not yet even begun to understand the darkest depths of their personal depravity. It is therefore very dangerous to suggest to a person that his bad thoughts and actions may be due to demonic influence. Such a suggestion [can] cause a disturbed person to become obsessed with the demonic.' VanderLugt goes on to say that the victim of demonic obsession could then 'exhibit the symptoms of false possession, in which he unconsciously imitates the symptoms of actual possession (including voice changes and apparent alterations of personality' ('What is Satan Doing? Satan is Possessing', http://www.gospelcom.net/rbc/ds/q1001/point5.html).

Leahy concludes that 'before there can be permanent *dispossession* of a demon there must be a spiritual *repossession* of the victim' (p. 104). He then goes on to show how that repossession takes place through the saving work of a Spirit-owned ministry of the word (Luke 10:1ff.). The preaching of Christ's word in the fullness of his Spirit is mightier than all the power of Satan (Luke 4:36). It is 'the power [*dunamis,* from which we derive 'dynamite'] of God unto salvation' (Rom. 1:16). Jesus faced Satan with the word of God; so must we.

Satan and today's Christians

Satan and his devils are also in continual conflict with God's people, tempting them and seeking to corrupt and destroy their lives, their faith, and their testimony (1 Cor. 5:5; 1 John 5:16).

True Christians have never denied Satan's existence. When God becomes real to a believer, Satan also becomes real. The conflict between the seed of the woman and the seed of the serpent prophesied in the Protoevangelium of Genesis 3:15 continues in the soul of each true believer. Each believer knows that struggle. Oh, what battles there are between the old and new man, flesh and spirit, nature and grace! Like Rebecca, whose twin babies warred within her womb, God's people often feel two seeds within them, struggling to break forth, until they cry out in desperation, 'Why am I thus?' (Gen. 25:22). Oh, what inexpressible struggles we have with the triple-headed enemy: Satan, the world, and the flesh! How torn we are by doubts, questions, unanswered riddles, unfulfilled promises, and satanic bruisings. No wonder our souls are often a mystery to us.

Before we knew Christ, we did not know such struggles. Only when we became believers could we understand this holy battle. God's people are intimately acquainted with Satan's daily attempts to bruise them. As a child of God, you are especially bruised when:

- Satan puts blasphemous thoughts into your mind, and then whispers that you cannot be a child of God if you have such thoughts.
- Satan gets you to question the truth of the promises of God and the mercy of that God who has never treated you ill.
- Satan seeks to persuade you that you have no part in the matter of salvation, for you have only begun with the Lord and not he with you.
- Satan argues with you that no child of God could be like you: so weak in faith, so corrupt, so hard and prayerless, so foolish and vain.

- Satan comes as your accuser, leading you to despair, or as an angel of light, leading you to presumption.
- Satan presents the world to you in fair colours, attempting to move you back into worldly customs, friendships, and vanities.
- Satan presses you to indulge in the lust of the flesh, the lust of the eyes, and the pride of life.

Bruised warriors often fear they are losing the battle against Satan. They wear themselves out in struggle, only to discover that they are sliding down the slope of sin toward destruction. At times, spiritual poverty and weakness threaten to overcome them. The tempter follows closely, bruising their heels. Like David, a bruised warrior cries with groans and pleadings, 'I shall one day perish by the hand of Saul' (1 Sam. 27:1). The hand of God appears hidden and the brink of hell visible. Voices within urge the exhausted believer to abandon his pursuit of God and his grace. Other voices condemn the believer, and justly so. Satan is a liar, but much of what he whispers to a believer about condemnation is sadly true. Conscience condemns. The law commands and curses. Divine justice is unsatisfied.

Bruised believers cannot walk with bruised heels. They can only fall if they do not recognise that they cannot help themselves. They must die to self-help. They must sign their own death sentence, admitting that God is righteous and just to cast them away for ever. In this they fear that Satan has not only won the skirmishes, but also the war.

Yet the amazing wonder of the gospel is that, despite a believer's self-condemnation, God gains the victory through the woman's seed, the victorious Christ. As Genesis 3:15 tells us, 'It [that is, the Seed, Christ] shall bruise thy head.'

Satan's heel-bruising is burdensome for a believer, but not fatal, for God overrules all the efforts of Satan for the good of his people. Through surrender of self comes victory in Christ. Christ gathers those whom Satan harasses. He shelters believers in his arms and says, as it were, 'Dear sheep, Satan may bruise your heels, but I have bruised Satan's head on your account through my death and resurrection, and through judgement.'

First, Christ bruised Satan's head in his atoning death. While Satan was bruising Christ's heel (his 'lower part', which is symbolic of his human nature) on Calvary, Christ was bruising the head of Satan (Gen. 3:15). The same heel that Satan bruised on Calvary was fatally bruising Satan, for at Calvary Christ made full payment for the sins of his elect. As Hebrews 2:14 says, 'Through death he might destroy him that had the power of death, that is, the devil' (cf. Col. 2:13-15).

In commenting on Genesis 3:15, John Phillips says, 'In his sentence of doom, Satan discovered that he had been too clever, after all. Seeking to avenge himself upon God for having cast him out of heaven, the evil one had opened the way for God to settle the mystery of iniquity once and for all. The very planet on which Satan had sought his vengeance would become the place for the final battle. And man himself would be the instrument of his defeat and doom, for God would become a man to accomplish that glorious end. The seed of the woman would put a final end both to sin and to Satan. Suddenly, the earth assumed an awesome significance in the universe' (*Exploring Genesis*, p. 61).

Second, Christ bruised Satan's head in his victorious resurrection. Satan could not keep Christ the Victor in the grave, for God's own Son would not see corruption. Christ rose from the grave. He appeared alive to believers for forty days, then ascended in triumph to his Father, leading captivity captive (Ps. 68:18). Christ is now in heaven at the right hand of the Father, beyond the reach of all the bruising powers of hell. The exalted Christ has the keys of death, hell, and the grave in his hand. The church is safe in Christ, for in him victory is assured.

Chapter 6

Satan's Future

The story is told of a chess champion who was fascinated by a painting of a chess game with two players in a European art gallery. One player was depicted as the devil, laughingly making what appeared to be a final move; the other, a young man, shaking and biting his nails. The title of the portrait was 'Checkmate'. The message was clear: the devil was about to capture the young man's soul for ever.

After studying the chessboard for hours, the chess champion realized that the move the devil was about to make would still leave a way of escape for the young man, and that he in turn could move to checkmate the devil. 'I wish you could hear me', the champion cried aloud to the young man. 'Though Satan has tricked you, you are not going to be checkmated. There is still one move left, and you can checkmate him. Your life can be transformed. You, not the devil, can have the last move.'

In Christ, believers shall have the last move against Satan. Shortly before Christ returns on the clouds, Satan will be 'loosed' for 'a little season' to launch a mighty onslaught against the church (Rev. 20:1-10). The believer may well fear that he will be checkmated by the arch-enemy, but Christ will then come as Victor to bruise fatally Satan's head in the final judgement. Christ will seize the old serpent Satan and cast him eternally into the bottomless pit of hell, which Christ himself describes as the lake of everlasting fire 'prepared for the devil and his angels' (Matt. 25:41).

Satan and his fallen angels dread this final judgement. Even when Jesus was here on earth, demons cowered before him, saying, 'What have we to do with thee? Didst thou come to destroy us?' (Mark 1:24). Luke 8:31 tells us that demons begged Jesus not to send them into 'the deep', or the abyss of hell. They knew that the abyss was their ultimate destination. Jude 6 also tells us that Christ has reserved everlasting chains for the evil spirits who rebelled in heaven.

J. Marcellus Kik writes, 'What a welcome will the Devil receive from those whom he has deceived! What curses, what vituperations, what abuses, what reviling, what berating will be heaped upon his head! He will be surrounded by a lake of curses. He will be hated, despised, and rejected throughout all eternity' (*An Eschatology of Victory,* p. 248).

What a comfort it is for believers to know that on Judgement Day, Satan and his seed will be cast out for ever. The bruising of Satan's head will become complete and final. The accuser of the brethren will never again bruise and accuse believers. He will never again trouble the seed of the woman. What a consolation to know that we fight a mortally wounded foe!

On Judgement Day, the suffering church of today will become the church triumphant. Believers will fully experience the spiritual essence of Exodus 14:13–14, 'Fear ye not, stand still, and see the salvation of the LORD, which he will shew to you to day: for the Egyptians whom ye have seen to day, ye shall see them again no more for ever. The LORD shall fight for you, and ye shall hold your peace.'

On Judgement Day, corruption will inherit incorruption (1 Cor. 15:50). All of the elect, from beginners to those advanced in grace, will be ushered into an everlasting Elim. Good will be walled in and evil walled out. Conflict will cease. Satan and his seed will be buried in the abyss of divine malediction.

Be of good courage, dear child of God. Christ's seed will not perish, despite all the efforts of Satan. Christ your Victor cannot fail. Satan has his limitations. 'The devil shall never lift his head higher than the saint's heel', William Gurnall wrote. Though extremely powerful, Satan and his demon host are not omnipotent, omniscient, or omnipresent. Satan simply cannot be everywhere at once. He is a fallen angel, not a fallen God; he is mighty, but not almighty.

Christ is the Almighty who will not forsake the work of his own hands. His cause is sure. His Second Advent is near. If you do not know Christ, be warned that when Satan is thrown into the everlasting lake of fire, unbelievers will perish with him. If you go to hell, you will be without a merciful God for ever and with a condemning Satan for ever. In hell you will find no relief from Satan's bruisings, no relief from the agonizing worm that dies not, no relief from the evil devices of the wicked one. As Hebrews 2:3 tells us, 'How shall we escape, if we neglect so great salvation?'

Let us remember that if Luther is right that the devil is God's devil, then hell is *God's* hell. Jesus Christ, not Satan, has the keys of hell. Dreadful will it be to fall into the hands of the living King of kings unprepared to meet him. To escape hell and be safe forever, we must belong to Christ's seed.

Are you Satan's seed or the seed of Christ? There is no other kind of seed. You either belong to Christ or Satan.

Make haste to answer that question. You still live in the day of grace, the time of salvation. Christ, the Seed of the woman, is still offered to you; yes, Christ offers himself to you. Pray for grace to receive God's gracious invitation, to bow under his word in holy surrender to him, and to grow in the grace and knowledge of Christ Jesus.

Let me close with two pieces of advice for when you feel the power of Satan in your life:

1. Flee to the Intercessor, Jesus Christ. He is the almighty Advocate, the perfect Paraclete, who promises to help you in every need. He is your only hope and your only stronghold. In Christ, Satan is defeated. Condemn yourself as Satan condemns you, but then come with all your unworthiness to your righteous Advocate before the Father.

2. Resist Satan with the word and promises of God. Do not bargain with Satan or give way to his enticements. Spurgeon wrote, 'Of two evils, choose neither. Learn to say "no." It will be of more use to you than to be able to read Latin.' Stand fast. Gird yourself with the armour of God. Resist Satan by showing God his own handwriting in his word. Remember that Satan is in chains and that you belong to Christ, who is mightier than Satan.

    Be sober, be vigilant, and hope to the end. Do not be self-confident or overly fearful, but stand guard against the seed of the serpent. Remember that Satan fell through pride and his goal will ever be to duplicate his sin in us by having us attempt to live independently of God, as if we were gods ourselves. Let us take heed lest we fall. Let us persevere in the faith and in humility before God. Let us remind ourselves that life is short and trials fleeting. Soon we will fly away and will then know the truth of Romans 16:20: 'And the God of peace shall bruise Satan under your feet shortly.' Commenting on this verse, Robert Haldane said, 'There were two victories to be obtained over Satan. By the first, his head was to be bruised under the feet of Jesus Christ; and by the second, the rest of his body will be bruised under the feet of believers.' Let these grand truths help you persevere in fighting Satan by the strength of our glorious Triune God.

Part Two
Knowing Satan's Weaknesses:
Fighting Him Defensively and Offensively

Chapter 7

Building an Unyielding Defence

'Stand therefore, having your loins girt about with truth,
and having on the breastplate of righteousness; and your
feet shod with the preparation of the gospel of peace;
above all, taking the shield of faith, wherewith ye shall
be able to quench all the fiery darts of the wicked. And
take the helmet of salvation...' (Ephesians 6:14-17a).

I once heard a story about a farmer who responded to water-melon thieves by putting a sign in his field that said: 'Warning: One of these melons has been poisoned.' For a few days, he thought his idea had worked: no more watermelons were stolen. Then, one day, he discovered that the sign had been altered to read: 'Warning: Two of these melons have been poisoned.' The farmer had to destroy his entire crop, as he didn't know which other melon was poisoned.

The devil works in similar ways. No matter what sign you put up, he changes it, and comes up with something better. He is a master manipulator and deceiver. How shall we ever fight against him successfully?

The eighteenth-century Scottish divine Ralph Erskine said the only choice we have in responding to Satan is 'flight or fight'. In light of that, the Christian soldier uses three major strategies to fight against Satan. The first we might call *strategic retreat,* or running for shelter to Christ. As Christian soldiers, we lean on the power of Christ's might, for we have no shelter from Satan but in Christ (Ps. 57:1).

Having learned where to find refuge in the evil day, we then use the second strategy of our military training, an *unyielding defence*. Much of Paul's famous spiritual warfare passage in Ephesians 6:10–18 describes this strategy against Satan. We stand, fight, conquer, and drive Satan out in the strength of God's armour.

The third strategy is an *attacking offence*. In Ephesians 6:14–18, Paul describes the five pieces of armour that we use defensively against Satan, then three ways to offensively fight him.

'Put on the whole armour of God' (Eph. 6:11), Paul tells us. Partial equipment will not suffice; twice we are told to put on the 'whole armour' (vv. 11a, 13a). We put on God by putting on his armour. Christ himself wore and made the armour, and the Holy Spirit fits it to us and makes it ours. We must fight through to the end until we hold the field against Satan. Then we must go on the offence, attacking him. Let's look at each of the eight pieces of armour that Paul counsels us to use, gleaning practical lessons for fighting Satan today.

The belt of truth

'Stand therefore, having your loins girt about with truth', Paul says in Ephesians 6:14. In Bible times, the girdle or belt, in physical warfare, was fastened or buckled at the waist around the short tunic worn by the soldier. The belt supported the 'loins' or muscles of the lower back and served as a foundation for much of his remaining armour. Both the breastplate and sword were attached to it. Thus, 'girt loins' symbolised readiness to do battle.

Loins girt with truth are a symbol of the Christian binding to himself the Christian faith revealed in the Bible. The Bible is our objective standard of truth and our final authority for doctrine and life. The Bible speaks of loins of the mind rather than loins of the heart (1 Pet. 1:13) because, before truth can get to the heart, it must pass through the mind. So if you would fend off Satan, you must first fill your mind with truth.

Truth in the mind is not sufficient, however. We must also possess knowledge of the truth in the heart, our inmost being.

44

If we are going to fight the devil successfully, not only must we master the truth, but the truth must master us.

Apart from God, Satan may be the most powerful mind in the universe. Human wisdom and reason is not sufficient to withstand Satan. But God's truth, as recorded in his word and personified in his Son, is more than sufficient to fight Satan.

We need truth to battle Satan. Without truth we will be 'tossed to and fro' with all kinds of doctrine. Many people today are ruled by their feelings. Despising the very theology they need, they are 'carried about with every wind of doctrine' (Eph. 4:14). Don't be tossed about with your emotions. Ground yourself in truth. Proverbs 23:23 teaches, 'Buy the truth and sell it not.' Or, as Thomas Brooks says in *Precious Remedies*, 'A man may lawfully sell his house, land and jewels, but truth is a jewel that exceeds all price, and must not be sold' (p. 21).

Jesus said, 'If ye continue in my word, ye shall be my disciples indeed, and ye shall know the truth, and the truth shall make you free' (John 8:31–32). We find freedom in Christ and in his truth. Demons can attack us, but they cannot overcome us if we are grounded in Christ and in his truth. The power of Christ's resurrection is greater than the power of Satan. Satan has no effective weapons against truth. He may rave against you and send numerous demons to hound you, but if you trust in Christ as the Truth of God, you will stand firm because your feet are planted on the Rock that cannot be moved.

Satan's first great weakness is that he is planted in a lie, and ultimately, a lie cannot stand against truth. Truth will triumph in the end. Cling to the truth. Know the truth, love the truth, and live the truth. Abide in Christ who is Truth, and you will gain the victory over Satan.

The Breastplate of Righteousness

The second piece of armour is the 'breastplate of righteousness' (6:14). In Paul's day, soldiers wore a protective breastplate made of metal or very tough leather. The breastplate covered the chest and the abdomen, protecting vital organs from swords and other weapons. The breastplate was a critical defence against mortal and lesser wounds.

People in Paul's day believed that organs such as the heart and the liver were the centre of affections. Emotions, such as joy or anger, originated in these organs. The apostle Paul used this understanding, unscientific though it was, to teach important spiritual lessons. He said believers must put on the breastplate of righteousness to protect the vital parts of the inner man and its faculties against the attacks of Satan. In their conflict with the invisible powers, believers are most vulnerable in their feelings and emotions. They need strong protection—a breastplate of righteousness—to keep from being wounded in their feelings and emotions.

The righteousness of the breastplate is provided by God in Christ. Christ earned that righteousness through his passive and active obedience. In passive obedience, Christ satisfied God's penal justice by fully paying the penalty of sin through his sufferings and death. In active obedience, he satisfied God's perfect demand that his holy law be kept flawlessly in order to merit eternal life. Only this combination of passive and active obedience was sufficient to fully satisfy God's justice. All other forms of righteousness are worthless.

Since no mere man can perform either aspect of this righteousness (for who can pay the eternal price of death and hell, and who can keep the law perfectly?), every sinner must depend on Christ to perform it for him. Christ can do this as a substitute for sinners, since he is also God. Being God, infinite value is attached to Christ's sufferings and his obedience to the law. Each one of us urgently and desperately needs to receive Christ's righteousness by Spirit-worked faith, for if we have this righteousness, we have forgiveness of sins and eternal life. If we lack this righteousness, we will perish in our sins.

Paul said that his great goal in life was to win Christ, 'and be found in him, not having mine own righteousness, which is of the law, but that which is through the faith of Christ, the righteousness of God which is by faith' (Phil. 3:9). Paul says, as it were,

'Everything else is dung, garbage. I used to be proud of my zeal and obedience. They were my breastplate; I relied on my own righteousness. But that is altogether different now.' Now, as the hymn says, 'My hope is built on nothing less/ Than Jesus' blood and righteousness.'

Have you learned to see your own righteousness as the filthy rags that Isaiah speaks of (64:6)? Are you clothed instead with the white-robed righteousness of Jesus Christ?

Satan schemes to keep us from resting in Christ's righteousness. He tries to get us to base our hope for salvation on our feelings. Then, when our feelings dissipate and grow lukewarm, Satan whispers: 'You are not a child of God—otherwise you wouldn't feel this way.'

It is easy to give way to Satan's suggestion to rely on our feelings, for feelings are an important part of true religion. True religion is more than notion; it also involves a person's will and emotions. We cannot be saved without feelings, but Satan exaggerates their importance. The righteousness of Christ is our protection against relying too much on feelings. As the hymn says:

> *I dare not trust the sweetest frame*
> *But wholly lean on Jesus' Name.*
> *On Christ, the solid Rock, I stand*
> *All other ground is sinking sand.*

Feelings are not the foundation of our salvation. Faith comes first. Feelings are the fruit of faith in Christ's righteousness. We must learn to cast ourselves on what Christ has done, and if we may do that by the grace of God, then we will experience feelings of joy and peace. We must not believe Satan's lie that faith is spun out of the web of our feelings. That is a dangerous, soul-damning, and hopeless task.

Shod feet
In verse 15 Paul tells us about the third piece of Christian armour: 'feet shod with the preparation of the gospel of peace'. A

good soldier needs proper footwear. The Roman soldiers, with whom Paul was well acquainted, wore sandals with strong straps. The sandals were thickly studded with sharp nails, which kept soldiers from slipping. Footwear was critical for fighting. The soldiers of Julius Caesar and Alexander the Great won many battles partly because of military shoes that prepared them for battle and allowed them to cover long distances in a short time, catching their enemies off guard.

Paul says that Christians must have the right footwear for battling against Satan, and this footwear is 'the preparation of the gospel of peace'. Christians must always be ready and prepared to do battle with the forces of Satan. Without the right footwear, a Christian will slip and slide to defeat. If a Christian enters the battle half-heartedly, not quite sure if it's worth the effort, he is already defeated. A believer must always be ready to fight and willing to endure hardship in the battle. A true soldier of Christ knows that the battle against Satan will be tough.

The gospel of peace is the pair of sandals with studs that enables the Christian to put his feet down and stand firm in battle. Like Luther, the Christian says, 'Here I stand', or like Paul, he says, 'Stand fast in the faith' (1 Cor. 16:13).

The best way to stand up to the devil is to have the clearest possible understanding of the gospel and to experience gospel peace that passes all understanding through the blood of Christ. Our identity, comfort, and stability depend on knowing the gospel intellectually and experientially. Then you can look Satan in the eye, and say, 'If God be for us, who can be against us?' You can say with assurance that 'the God of peace shall bruise Satan under your feet shortly' (Rom. 16:20).

The shield of faith
The fourth piece of armour is the shield of faith. Paul says this shield enables the believer to 'quench all the fiery darts of the wicked' (v. 16). Roman shields in Paul's day were about four feet long by two feet wide, large enough to cover most of the body. They had fireproof metal coverings, which was important

to minimize the effect of flaming arrows. With this shield, a soldier could not only stop fiery darts and flaming arrows, but also extinguish them.

Satan's devices are like fiery darts and flaming arrows. Satan has thousands of ways to attack believers with his darts, including blasphemous thoughts about God, sinful suggestions, and corrupt desires. He shoots darts outwardly at believers as well as inwardly at their hearts and minds. We need the shield of faith to withstand Satan's assaults for these reasons:

1. Faith helps us recognize satanic devices. William Gurnall says, 'Faith looks behind the curtain of sense, and sees sin before it is dressed up for the stage.' Faith sees the ugliness and hellishness of sin without its camouflage.

2. Faith puts Christ between Satan and us. Christ's blood is the fireproof covering in our shield of faith. Christ's blood and righteousness intervene between Satan and us, guarding us against Satan's fiery attacks.

Our biggest problem in battling Satan is that we forget to hold up the shield of faith. If you're a believer, raise high the shield of faith. Hide behind Christ. He will take the blows of Satan for you. He has already warded off every fiery dart to be your perfect Saviour. Trust him. He will never leave you nor forsake you.

Satan's goal is to push aside your shield, then stab you under your armour. Do not let him do that. Take good care of your shield by living in faith. Rest in the person of Christ—come, hear, see, trust, take, know, embrace, rejoice, love, triumph in Christ. By faith, lay hold of Christ, surrendering every part of yourself. Cling to him the way the prongs of a ring cling to its diamond. Rely on his promises. Faith honours Christ, makes us strong, comforts us, makes us useful, and guarantees Satan's defeat.

It is said, 'No battle was ever planned by hell's most gifted strategist which can conquer faith. All its inflamed and terrible darts fall harmless as they strike against the shield of faith.'

Failing to use faith as a shield—that is, to walk in unbelief—is sure to be dangerous, if not fatal. Unbelief dishonours us, weakens us, destroys our comfort, and prevents our usefulness. Deny your doubts; quench your questionings. Refuse to surrender to your daily lusts. Battle Satan with the shield of faith. Trust in the Lord at all times. Remember, a faith that never withstands hell's temptations will not take you to heaven's rewards.

The helmet of salvation
'And take the helmet of salvation' (6:17a). The helmet of salvation is a critical piece of armour. No matter how well a soldier's body is protected, if his head is left uncovered, his chance of survival is minimal. A soldier must wear his helmet.

When an enemy is spotted in battle today, soldiers are ordered to take their battle stations. The first thing a soldier does after positioning himself behind a gun is to put his steel helmet on for protection from enemy shells or shrapnel.

The Roman helmet of Paul's day was a leather cap covered with plates of metal. It was adorned with a kind of ornamental crest or plume. First Thessalonians 5:8 tells us that this helmet is 'the hope of salvation'.

Discouragement is a common ploy of Satan. Satan wants Christians to think that they have been battling Satan for a very long time and that they have made very little headway in the fight. They stumble into sin every day to the point where there seems to be little point in going on. 'My struggle against sin is useless', they tell themselves. 'My attempt to live a holy life is hopeless. It is of no use to serve God.'

Satan digs in, tempting believers to become deserters in Christ's army. The only answer for this fiery dart is our hope of future salvation, or, as Romans 8 tells us, our 'hope of glory'. Salvation in the past is justification, salvation in the present is sanctification, and salvation in the future is glorification. Glorification is what Paul has in mind here.

When Satan makes you feel like giving up in the battle against sin, put on your helmet of hope, Paul says. Believe that you have been saved, you are being saved, and you shall be saved. Cling to your only hope, Jesus Christ (1 Tim. 1:1), who is the same yesterday, today, and for ever. By his resurrection, you are newly born to a living hope (1 Pet. 1:3–4) and will abundantly increase in hope through the Holy Spirit (Rom. 15:13).

One object of this abounding hope is the ultimate blessedness of God's kingdom (Acts 2:26; Tit. 1:2). Hope produces joyful confidence in God (Rom. 8:28), patience in tribulation (Rom. 5:3), and perseverance in prayer. It anticipates actual righteousness (Gal. 5:5) and is thus good, blessed, and glorious (2 Thess. 2:16; Tit. 2:13; Col. 1:27). It anchors the soul by linking it to God's steadfastness in Christ (Heb. 3:6; 6:18–19).

If you are a Christian, you have a wonderful future. Your salvation cannot be taken from you. So look to the future. Look to glory, and do not lose heart.

In Romans 8:29–30, which describes the process of salvation from eternity past to eternity future, Paul speaks of glorification in the past tense: 'For whom he did foreknow … them he also glorified.' Paul speaks of the future event of heavenly glorification as if it has already happened because his hope for the future is inseparably tied with what God has done for him in the past. The chain of salvation cannot be broken. Every link is anchored in God's eternal, predestinating love. Predestination, calling, faith, justification, sanctification, and glorification are all linked together.

Dear believer, be of good hope. No one can pluck you from the Father's hand, nor from Christ's hand (John 10:28–29). The Saviour who persevered for you in the thick of battle will give you hope to stay the course in his strength. By wearing the helmet of hope, you will be prepared for every battle with Satan. Christ will sustain you in the fight and will bring you victory. When you see the enemy Satan coming, run to your battle station and put on the helmet of hope. That is the only way to survive.

Lift up your head; let hope be your ornament, your plume of eternal victory. The coming of the Son of man draws near. Soon you will no longer need your helmet. Your battle will be over.

Satan will be eternally crushed. You will reign with the Captain of your salvation. You will come out of the great tribulation, wearing robes made white in Christ's blood. You will stand before the throne of God, praising the Lamb of God. The Lamb will lead you to living fountains of water; you will forever bask in his smile, bathe in his glory, and feast in his presence. You will find communing with Christ to be the essence of heaven. You will eternally rejoice in knowing, seeing, loving, praising, and glorifying him.

Do you hope in Jesus Christ? Everyone hopes in something; we cannot live without hope. But do you have the sure hope of the true Christian? Are you abounding in hope? Do you think often of the hope of heaven? You will fight Satan feebly if you view heaven dimly. But if hope is your helmet, you will be protected against blows to your head. You will withstand the crushing discouragement of the evil one.

Chapter 8

Building an Attacking Offence

*'Take...the sword of the Spirit, which is the word of God:
praying always with all prayer and supplication in the
Spirit, and watching thereunto with all perseverance and
application for all saints'* (Ephesians 6:17b-18).

In January of 2002, when I returned to my flat after lecturing on
the doctrine of salvation in an eastern European country, I was
assaulted by two men who knocked me down, tied and gagged
me, ran a knife up and down my back, all the while shouting,
'Mafia, mafia!' God graciously spared me and comforted me im-
measurably with his word throughout this 45-minute ordeal, but
you can understand that I considered myself a dead man.

The Mafia is not always so blatantly or aggressively open,
however. More often than not, they, like Satan, run a camouflaged
organization and operation. Do you know the addresses of Mafia
leaders? Do you recognize them beneath their business suits and
their apparently legitimate businesses? We know that the Mafia
controls money-laundering businesses, various rings of prostitu-
tion, and all kinds of crime, but it is difficult to pin them down.
In last night's paper, I read that one of the Mafia's leaders was
so slippery that although there were more than a dozen charges
against him, the jury acquitted him and he will soon be set free.

Satan's spiritual Mafia controls people and nations—sometimes openly and blatantly, but more often in a camouflaged way.
We need much wisdom and strength, not only to defend ourselves against his attacks, but also to offensively search him out
and go on the attack in the strength of our God. Paul goes on in

Ephesians 6:17b-18 to tell us how to do that, presenting us with three powerful weapons in our battle against the arch-enemy of our Saviour.

The sword of the Spirit

The sword of the Spirit, which is the word of God (6:17b) is a unique piece of armour in fighting Satan, for it attacks the enemy as well as repels him. God magnifies his word by using it as a double-edged sword (Heb. 4:12). The Holy Spirit, the author of God's 'breathed-out' word, enables us to interpret and use this word. Here is how the sword of the Spirit can be used to combat Satan:

1. It is a defence against Satan. Jesus sets the example here. He responded each time to Satan's temptations in the desert with 'It is written' (Matt. 4:1–11). His words from Scripture plunged like steel into the heart of Satan. That is how we, too, need to respond to Satan. Hand-to-hand combat with Satan and with temptation seldom works. We need the sword of the Spirit in our hand.

    Satan cannot defeat a believer who by faith wields the promises of the Bible. Faith trusts in the promises of God. When Satan says, 'You will one day fall at my hand', faith says, 'No', and lifts up the word of God as a sword, saying, 'I am persuaded that he that hath begun a good work in me will perform it until the day of Jesus Christ' (cf. Phil. 1:6). When Satan hurls the doubt, 'Your sin is too great', faith responds by saying, 'He is able also to save to the uttermost them that come unto God by him' (Heb. 7:25). For every dart of Satan, God has provided a sure defence in his word. 'The only way to overcome Satan', Calvin wrote, 'is by keeping to the word of God in its entirety.'

2. It is an offensive weapon against Satan. We fight Satan by finding shelter in Christ. We fight him with an unyielding defence. But we also fight Satan by taking the offence against him. The sword of the Spirit, which is the word of God, gives

us clear directions, powerful motives, rich encouragements, and instructive examples that equip us well for confronting Satan.

Do not live by bread alone, but by every word of God. Intimately acquaint yourself with the Bible by studying and memorizing it daily. That will help keep God's sword sharp in your hand. Keep that sword polished and bright by living the Bible's truths each day. Keep the sword ready at all times through constant prayer. Speak out; bear witness to Scripture truth. Carry the light of God's word into a dark world, shining its light into every dark corner.

Ask for the wisdom of the Holy Spirit to wield the sword of Scripture against Satan. The Spirit is the ultimate author and interpreter of God's word, so seek his wisdom. The Spirit delights to open our minds to his word. He will teach us how to use it as a sword against Satan.

To the blind, the Bible is an ordinary book, full of mistakes. In the hand of the Spirit, the Bible is supernatural power. Hebrews 4:12 says that the word of God 'is quick and powerful and sharper than any two-edged sword, piercing even to the dividing asunder of soul and spirit.' When you use God's word with skill against demonic attack, Satan will feel the sword of the Spirit penetrate his joints and marrow, cutting away his strength and all his wisest plans.

In dependence on the Spirit, use the sword of the Bible to stand your ground against Satan, to assail him, to run at him, to rout him, and to drive him from the field. Have confidence in the word of God. It will never fail you, not even in the thick of battle with Satan (Apollyon), as Bunyan so poignantly tells of Christian while in the valley of humiliation:

> But as God would have it, while Apollyon was fetching his last blow, thereby to make a full end of this good man, Christian nimbly stretched forth his hand for his sword, and caught it, saying, "Rejoice not against me, O mine enemy: when I fall I

shall arise"; and with that gave him a deadly thrust, which made him give back, as one that had received his mortal wound. Christian, perceiving that, made at him again, saying, "Nay, in all these things we are more than conquerors through him that loved us." And with that Apollyon spread forth his dragon wings, and sped him away.

Praying in the Spirit

'Praying always with all prayer and supplication in the Spirit' (6:18a). Prayer is the second offensive weapon against Satan. Martin Luther said, 'Prayer is a strong wall and fortress of the church; it is a godly Christian's weapon.' John Bunyan said, 'The greatest weapon in the storehouse of God is the weapon of prayer.'

Prayer is critical because every piece of Christian armour is useless without it. Prayer is like oil. Just as every part of an engine is useless without oil, so every part of Christian warfare is vain without prayer. Fighting Satan without prayer is like David fighting Goliath in Saul's armour. The armour doesn't fit, and it is ineffective against the blows of the enemy.

In withstanding Satan through prayer, Paul tells us to do the following:

1. *Pray always.* Some generations ago, several ministers gathered in the Scottish highlands to discuss what it meant to 'pray without ceasing' (1 Thess. 5:17). After considerable discussion, one minister asked a little maid girl if she knew what it meant.

   'Yes, sir', she said. 'As I arose this morning from bed, I prayed that the Sun of righteousness would arise with healing in his wings over me today. When I got dressed, I prayed that I might be clothed with Christ's righteousness. As I dusted the furniture in this room before you arrived, I prayed that the Lord would wipe my heart clean through the blood of Jesus. When I made your refreshments ready, I prayed that

Jesus Christ would be my food and drink. Sir, I pray my way through each day, for prayer is my breath, my life.'

Praying without ceasing means praying at set times and seasons as well as sending up short petitions to God throughout the day. It means praying at stated times of prayer and praying whenever you feel the least impulse to do so. Praying is more important than whatever else you are doing. Spurgeon said, 'We must addict ourselves to prayer.'

2. *Pray with prayer and supplication.* Though Paul appears to be repeating himself in Ephesians 6:18, he is not. Paul is saying, 'Pray with heartfelt, pleading prayer. Truly pray in your prayer.' Tragically, we often fail miserably in using the weapon of prayer. Satan can doze beside our prayerless prayers.

The marginal notes on James 5:17 in the King James Version of the Bible say that Elijah 'prayed in his prayer'. That means the prophet truly prayed with all his heart. Samuel Rutherford said that the condition of the heart in prayer is more important than the words that are said. He wrote, 'A dumb beggar gets more when he can't talk than when he can. Tears have a tongue, a grammar, and a language that the Lord can understand better than words.' Bunyan put it this way, 'It is better when thou prayest, to rather let thy heart be without words, than thy words without heart.'

3. *Pray with all prayer.* That means praying while acknowledging God in all your ways and trusting that he will direct all your paths (Prov. 3:5–6). Bring all your needs to God, great and small. As Mary Winslow told her son, 'Tell the Lord everything about you, as if he knew nothing about you, yet knowing that he knows all things.' Entrust yourself and all of your needs into God's all-sufficient hands, if you would defeat Satan on things small and large.

4. *Pray in the Spirit.* Romans 8:26 says that the Holy Spirit

helps us to pray in our infirmities and intercedes for us with groanings that cannot be uttered. The Holy Spirit shows us how miserable we are by nature and how great our debt is to God. The Spirit also enables us to think saving thoughts of God, of Christ, and of blessed things. He grants us faith and helps us express our needs and thoughts in prayer. He keeps us from hypocrisy, coldness, and all that is unseemly.

Let me illustrate how the Holy Spirit does this. A small boy was being taught by his father how to steer a ship. As the boy began to steer, his father stood directly behind him. The father knew that if he didn't help his son, the boat would crash on the rocks or be swept away in the swift current. The father did not push his son aside, though, telling him it would be better for the father to take the helm. He leaned over his son, put his hands upon his son's hands, and then guided his son's hands on the wheel. Through the father's guidance the son steered the ship to safety.

Likewise, my friends, we pray best when the Spirit grips our hearts and guides our thoughts, steering us in the course that he has charted for us. Just as this boy could not steer the ship on his own, so we cannot pray rightly without the Holy Spirit. Let us have confidence in him and seek to be filled with him (Eph. 5:18).

Martyn Lloyd-Jones said, 'Everything we do in the Christian life is easier than prayer.' If you desire to pray in the Spirit to fight Satan, do the following:

- Lean on Christ. In him all prayer is made effective.
- Make prayer a priority. Bunyan said, 'You can do more than pray after you've prayed, but you can't do more than pray until you've prayed.'
- Find sweetness in prayer. When I was nine years old, my dad told me, 'Always remember that a true believer has a place to go—the throne of grace. Prayer is God's gift to go to himself. He is a prayer-giving, a prayer-hearing, and a prayer-answering God.'

William Bridge said, ''Tis a mercy to pray, though I [may] never receive the mercy prayed for.' Joseph Hall put it this way: 'Good prayers never come weeping back, for I am sure I shall receive either what I ask or what I should be asking for.'

- Repeat God's promises. God is the tender of his own word. Take him at his word. He will make prayer effective for you.

If Satan rests content beside us because he knows that we lack the breath and vitality of genuine prayer, our prayer will be powerless against him. We must use what Bunyan called 'the weapon of all-prayer'. If we believe that man is man and God is God, we must be persistent in praying in our prayers.

Watch with perseverance

'Watching thereunto with all perseverance and supplication for all saints' (6:18b). The true soldier must stand guard at his post; he must be vigilant, watchful, and alert. Likewise, the soldier of Christ must watch and pray to ward off the attacks of Satan.

Paul brings praying and watching together in one verse (6:18b) because they are truly inseparable. Our day often goes poorly because we have failed to begin our day in heartfelt prayer. We also pray poorly as we retire in the evening because we haven't been watchful through the day. 'Watch and pray', Jesus said (Matt. 26:41).

The devil loves to work with drowsy Christians. The foolish virgins missed welcoming the Bridegroom because their lamps ran out of oil. In *Pilgrim's Progress*, Bunyan's Christian lost his roll, symbolizing his assurance of faith, when he fell asleep.

We can defeat Satan only if we watch and pray. We do this by:

- *Being constantly aware.* We must be aware of what is going on in our hearts and in the hearts of our family and our home. We must be aware of the needs of our church and the children of God. We must be aware of the needs of our city, state, and nation. We must be aware of what is happening in the government and world affairs. We must broaden our sense of awareness, for that will give us more material for intercession.

- *Interceding for others.* We should pray for ministers and the progress of the gospel. Paul pleads for that in verses 19–20. We should also make 'supplication for all saints' (v. 18b). We are never more like Christ than when we are engaged in heartfelt intercession. T. J. Bach said that many of us cannot reach the mission field on our feet, but we can reach it on our knees. Intercession delivers us from selfishness, which Satan so delights to see; it lifts us above ourselves, gives us joy in service, and enables us to keep Satan at bay.

- *Persevering.* The Greek word used here for *perseverance* means to pursue until you get your prey. Press on as you watch, remembering that 'In due season we shall reap if we faint not' (Gal. 6:9). Keep knocking on the door of God's grace. Don't leave after one knock, like a disheartened salesman. Be like Mercy in Bunyan's *Pilgrim's Progress,* who kept knocking to the point of fainting until God answered her. Watch for God's answers. Do not turn your back on him.

- *Watching in all things.* That is what Paul commanded Timothy (2 Tim. 4:5). Obey the calling: 'Let everyone that nameth the name of Christ, depart from iniquity' (2 Tim. 2:19). As E. M. Bounds writes, '"Watch" is the keynote of safety. [We must be] wide awake not only when we see his form and fear his presence, but wide awake to see him when he is not to be seen, to repel him when he comes in any one of his ten thousand guises or disguises—this is our wise and safe course' (*Satan: His Personality, Power and Overthrow,* p. 144).

Stand up for Jesus

Paul's well-outfitted soldier in Ephesians 6:14–18 gives us a comprehensive picture of how to fight against Satan. In dependency on the Spirit, and in Christ's strength, use each piece of armour prayerfully every day, remembering what Samuel Rutherford said: 'Satan is only God's master fencer to teach us to use our weapons.' Don't let any pieces of God's weaponry hang in the back of your closet unused. You need every one. Trust God to help you; don't lean upon your own understanding. As Calvin warned, 'If we contend with Satan according to our own view of things, he will a hundred times overwhelm us and we will never be able to resist.'

Look to Christ, remembering that he wore the weapons of Ephesians 6 himself, as Isaiah already points out in the Old Testament:

> The *Messiah* girds his loins with the truth, by fearing God and walking in the power and wisdom of the Spirit (Is. 11:5). The *LORD God* puts on the breastplate of righteousness to deliver his people from bondage to sins (59:17). The *LORD* himself comes—his feet shod—bearing good news of peace to those captivated in sin and judgment (52:7). The *LORD* himself is the shield behind which faith takes refuge from enemies. The *LORD* wears the helmet of salvation as he brings deliverance from the power of sin and gives his Spirit and word (59:17). The sword of the Spirit is God's word and proceeds from the mouth of the *Messiah*, the Servant who will deliver the nations from the power of darkness (49:2). Prayer is the way all this happens, for prayer relies on the Lord (Powlison, *Power Encounters,* p. 114).

As a believer in Christ, put your spiritual warfare into Christ's hands. Remember that ultimately the battle against Satan is not yours but his (2 Chron. 20:15). Jesus Christ will not lose the battle against the Prince of this world. You are part of his body, the church, and he will not relinquish his bride.

Take heart, soldier. Your comforts are many. You are in a

strong position, being 'in Christ'. You have all the equipment you need—the whole armour of God. You have the help of a Master Warrior, David's own Teacher and Guide, the Holy Spirit (Pss. 18, 144). He makes the devil be your 'polisher, while he intends to be [your] destroyer', wrote Stephen Charnock. You have the promise of help in the evil day and victory guaranteed at the last day. You are on the winning side; ultimately, as William Gurnall wrote, 'God sets the devil to catch himself.' You may lose some skirmishes to Satan, but through Christ Jesus, you will win the war.

> *Stand up, stand up for Jesus;*
> *Stand in his strength alone.*
> *The arm of flesh will fail you,*
> *You dare not trust your own.*
> *Put on the gospel armour,*
> *Each piece put on with prayer.*
> *Where duty calls or danger,*
> *Be never wanting there.*

Let us pray with a Puritan:

> O thou whose very promise is balm,
>   every touch life,
>   draw near to thy weary warrior,
>   refresh me, that I may rise again to wage the strife,
>   and never tire until my enemy is trodden down.
> Give me such fellowship with thee that I may defy Satan,
>   unbelief, the flesh, the world...
> Give me a draught of the eternal fountain
>   that lieth in thy immutable, everlasting love and decree.
> Then shall my hand never weaken, my feet never stumble,
>   my sword never rest, my shield never rust,
>   my helmet never shatter, my breastplate never fall,
>   as my strength rests in the power of thy might.
>   (*Valley of Vision,* p. 181)

Part Three
Knowing Satan's Strategies:
His Devices and Their Remedies

Chapter 9

Satan's Strategies and Skill

In his book, *Satanism*, Bruce Frederickson writes, 'In the story of the Trojan horse, rather than attack the city of Troy directly, Greek soldiers built a huge, hollow, wooden horse. They left it in front of the gates of the city of Troy. Thinking the horse a gift, the Trojans wheeled it inside the city walls to admire it. After the Trojans fell asleep, the Greeks crept out of their hiding place inside the horse and took the city by surprise. Satan often operates like that—he attacks from behind [and from within] where he is least expected.'

We encounter Satan's strategies and devices most when we experience God most, for Satan loathes seeing a true Christian commune with God. As Luther said, 'For where God builds a church, there the devil builds a chapel. Thus is the devil even God's ape'—that is, imitator.

The Puritans, who experienced great intimacy with God, became greatly familiar with the strategies and devices of Satan. They wrote frequently and with great depth on spiritual warfare. In this section of the book, I want to bring together in contemporary language the cream of what six Puritan authors said about Satan's devices and their remedies in the following works:

- Thomas Brooks's *Precious Remedies Against Satan's Devices,* a well-known classic that has often been reprinted by Banner of Truth Trust
- Richard Gilpin's *A Treatise on Satan's Temptations,* a 500-page classic recently reprinted by Soli Deo Gloria
- William Spurstowe's *The Wiles of Satan,* a rare but helpful

little work, recently reprinted by Soli Deo Gloria

- John Downame's *The Christian Warfare,* a massive two-volume work of 1,800 pages, which has not been reprinted since the seventeenth century
- William Gurnall's *The Christian in Complete Armour,* a detailed work on Ephesians 6:10–20, reprinted by Banner of Truth Trust
- Thomas Goodwin's *A Child of Light Walking in Darkness,* which has a most helpful section on Satan's activity in our spiritual darkness (*Works of Goodwin,* 3:256–288)

I will address three questions: First, what do *strategies, devices,* and other related terms mean? Second, why is Satan so skilled at tempting us? Third, what are some of Satan's major strategies and devices, and what remedies does God provide for us in battling against them?

The terms, *strategies* and *devices*

This week my family has an unknown number of families living with us—families of mice. My wife and I are approaching this relatively calmly and rationally. We have established four concentric circles. First, the outermost circle is our *goal*: remove all mice from our home. The next, somewhat smaller concentric circle is our *strategy* or *plan*: get a variety of traps to catch the mice. Presently our home is littered with snap traps, poisonous traps, and sticky traps. A third more focused circle calls us to use a variety of *devices* or bait to catch the mice, ranging from cheese to peanut butter, to entice them to fall prey to our strategy. Finally, the innermost circle consists of *remedies*: carry the dead mice in the snap traps outside to dispose of them; carry the caught but still living mice outside on the sticky traps and kill them (my least favourite approach, as I shrink from killing anything); or dispose of the dead remains of poisoned mice, if and when they can be found (my wife's least favourite approach, as she doesn't like the idea of unfound, dead mice lying about). So far, we've removed four mice from our home, but, I'm afraid, have a long way to go.

Satan treats us like these mice, only his mission of four concentric circles is more complex. His largest circle of *goals* (also called purposes or objectives), all of which are designed to injure God's glory, is at least fourfold: (1) to destroy us because we bear God's image, (2) to overthrow the kingdom of God, (3) to retain control of what he still possesses, and (4) to regain his lost territory. Those goals have already been addressed in some measure, so we will not delve into them further now; in this address, we want to become more focused.

The second, somewhat smaller circle represents Satan's *strategies* or *plans*. The term *strategy* refers to the science of generalship, or to leading an army. It is an all-encompassing term, but can also be used of specific plans or traps for a war or campaign. Satan has many traps to use, including snap traps, poisonous traps, and sticky traps. In this section of the book, we're going to look closely at four of his many strategies: Satan strategises to entice us to sin, to hinder our spiritual disciplines, to misrepresent God and truth, and to oppose our sanctification.

The third, more focused circle is Satan's *devices* by which he carries out his strategies and goals. The term *devices* (Greek: *noema*) suggests the thoughts and actions involved in deceiving someone, such as ambushes in war, fake moves in a sport, or fallacies in a debate. In 2 Corinthians 2:11 Paul provides guidance to the church in Corinth for handling an incestuous person 'lest Satan should get an advantage of us: for we are not ignorant of his devices'. Paul warns the Corinthians not to let Satan get the upper hand over them by making them so zealous against the sin of the incestuous person that they would reject his sincere repentance. Then the man would be overwhelmed with sorrow and Satan would outwit them.

Thus, Paul was not ignorant of Satan's strategy to destroy the church of Corinth. Satan's first device was to encourage laxity of discipline, and so all manner of disorders broke out (cf. 1 Corinthians). When the church repented, Satan's next device was to promote a harsh, unforgiving kind of church discipline. All along, Satan had the same strategy, but used different devices.

Paul warns against an abuse of church discipline, lest Satan thereby accomplish his strategy for the Corinthian church.

The term *devices* has several synonyms, of which I'll just mention the three most important. One biblical synonym is *wiles,* from the Greek *methodeia*, and the source of our English word *method.* Both of its New Testament occurrences are in Ephesians (4:14; 6:11) and indicate a negative, cunning method that involves scheming. Some translations of Ephesians 6:11 use 'the schemes of the devil' rather than 'the wiles of the devil'. Another synonym, *stratagem,* is only a part of a plan or strategy; it refers to a ploy or dirty trick that always involves deception. Hence, devices, wiles, schemes, and stratagems all carry the same meaning.

Finally, there is the innermost circle, the *remedies*. Here is where my mice analogy breaks down, because we need to outfox Satan by implementing the biblical remedies that God provides, so that Satan does not carry us away to hell to destroy us for ever.

We now want to focus on the inner circles of Satan's strategies and devices and their remedies. William Spurstowe warned us, 'Satan is full of devices, and studies arts of circumvention by which he unweariedly seeks the irrecoverable ruin of the souls of men' (p. 6). Just as it is essential for military leaders to record the strategies and devices of an enemy in war, so it is essential for true Christians to acquaint themselves with their enemy, Satan, and his methods of doing battle. We need to study the strategies and devices that Satan uses today to be able to think through and act upon God's scriptural remedies.

Satan's skill at tempting
Before we look at Satan's devices, however, we need to ask: What makes Satan so skilful at tempting us to sin through various devices? William Spurstowe provides the following six reasons:

1. *Satan's spiritual being and intellectual power.* When people tempt each other, they do so with overt actions. For example,

Joseph tempted his brothers' devotion to their youngest brother, Benjamin, by asking his steward to hide his cup in Benjamin's sack. But Satan, who is a spirit, doesn't have to use overt actions. He can prey directly on the mind, tempting us to yield to his devices. Satan could enter the heart of Judas Iscariot and tempt the disciple to betray Christ (John 13:2). Satan could enter the heart of Ananias and tempt him to lie to the Holy Ghost (Acts 5:3).

Satan, though fallen, is still an angel, so he is intellectually far superior to us. That makes him very dangerous. Jonathan Edwards said, 'The devil was educated in the best divinity school in the universe, viz., the heaven of heavens.' Calvin called him 'an acute theologian'. In addition, this fallen angel is able to hide his deadly intellectual poison under 'a beautiful and shining skin'. Satan's great intellect and cunning deceit should make us especially wary, for we know that we cannot defeat him through our limited intellectual abilities (Spurstowe, *The Wiles of Satan,* p. 14).

2. *Satan's experience and work.* The devil is old but not infirm. His temptations are like the arrows of a skilful archer that seldom fail to hit their target (Jer. 50:9). Over the centuries he has mastered the art of wickedness. Satan knows by experience when the best time is to shoot his arrows. He knows what bait to use whenever he fishes. He tempts young people with beauty, the thrifty with money, and the ambitious with power. William Jenkyn says, 'He has an apple for Eve, a grape for Noah, a change of raiment for Gehazi, and a bag for Judas.' He has remarkable experience in overcoming every defence against yielding to his temptations.

Satan knows how to disguise sin by giving it a false complexion. Spurstowe says that just as Apelles painted only one side of King Antigonus's face to conceal the side that had no eye, so Satan paints the half-face of sin.

Satan is adept at deflecting our defences. Believers are often startled and perplexed when they are tempted because

Satan responds so quickly and effectively to their arguments against sinning. Satan's rapid response ought to teach us to totally and immediately deny him rather than dispute with him.

Satan's experience helps him to confidently assault the holiest believers. If Satan cannot keep believers out of heaven, he will do what he can to keep heaven out of believers here on earth. As Spurstowe says: 'If not to extinguish their light, yet [Satan tempts] to eclipse their lustre; if not to cause a shipwreck, yet to raise a storm; if not to hinder their happy end, yet to molest them in their way' (p. 21).

Satan is a confident, experienced adversary. Who has wrestled with him without being wounded? If great men like Noah, Lot, David, and Peter fell under Satan's temptations, how can we hope to withstand the Tempter? Do not presume that you can defeat the devil in your own strength.

3. *Satan's tireless energy for promoting evil.* Satan relentlessly and endlessly tempts man to keep him from God. Satan has a one-track mind. That single-minded purpose makes him formidable. An ancient Italian proverb says, 'Lord, deliver me from a man who has but one business to do.'

Satan tempts us to be idle, but he is never idle. Spurstowe writes, 'How hard it is to persuade men that to walk circumspectly is a duty, or that to be diligent in their callings is one of the best antidotes to preserve the soul from the putrefaction of lusts, and to fence it against the incursions of an assiduous tempter!' (p. 25).

4. *Satan has a kingdom of demons.* Daniel 7:10 says that 'thousand thousands' of angels minister to God, and 'ten thousand times ten thousand' stand before him. Fallen angels who serve Satan are also numerous, since Scripture describes Satan and his demons as a powerful kingdom. Paul implies that the number of fallen angels is great when he says that we wrestle against 'principalities, against powers, against the

rulers of the darkness of this world, against spiritual wickedness in high places' (Eph. 6:12).

Satan's kingdom is also united in purpose. Every demon
hates God's glory and our happiness. Every demon unitedly promotes Satan's doctrine, Satan's distinctions, Satan's
domination, and Satan's distractions. Every demon unitedly
opposes God's position, God's precepts, God's purity, and
God's people. There are no divisions in Satan's kingdom
(Matt. 12:26), no uprisings because of poor pay, no com-
plaints about strenuous marches, no baulking at difficult
tasks. We expect the angels in heaven who dwell with the
Triune God to be united. But is it not remarkable that the
devils in hell are more united in purpose than the church on
earth? What a tragedy that the communion of devils so often
exceeds the communion of saints.

If devils are filled with pride, wrath, envy, and bitterness,
how can they be so united? Just as enemies on earth can be
united through mutual hatred of a third party, so Satan's demons are united by their mutual hatred of God and man. As
good angels rejoice over the repentance of a sinner, evil angels rejoice over the destruction of a sinner. Spurstowe says,
'Ruined sinners are the only trophies and spoils of hell' (p.
29).

5. *Satan's evil suggestions, which are nearly indistinguishable
from our own corrupt desires.* It is difficult at times to know
whether a sinful thought originates with Satan or with us.
It is difficult to distinguish between evil that is sown in the
mind by the Tempter and evil that is ours by nature. As the
old saying goes: 'The devil's boots don't creak.' Spurstowe
says that a bird will hatch an egg and nourish a young bird
until it discovers that the young one is not its own. Then the
mother bird pushes the intruder out of the nest. Likewise, if
we would recognise promptings as those given by Satan, we
would have the strength to repudiate them. If King David had
known that Satan was tempting him to number the people of

Israel, he undoubtedly would have stopped counting immediately (1 Chron. 21:1).

6. *Satan's skill at matching his suggestions with our own corrupt reason.* Satan cannot conquer our soul by force; his success depends on confusing us about the origin of his suggestions. 'The devil may allure, God alone can effectually
change, but none can compel us' (p. 33).

Satan is a master at suggesting that we believe what we
want to believe rather than believe the truth. To the athe-
ist, Satan suggests that worshipping God is a crutch for the
weak-minded. To the convicted, Satan suggests that a little
religion will do. To the nominal Christian, Satan suggests
that intellectual faith is sufficient. To the true believer, Satan
suggests that the worldly do not suffer as the righteous do
(Ps. 73).

Spurstowe concludes, 'If Satan, who is the evil seedman,
scatters any seeds of temptations, to which the heart is as
a prepared and disposed soil by the corrupt principles that
lodge in it, they will quickly sprout forth into acts, and grow
into a root that will bear gall and wormwood' (p. 35).

Chapter 10

Confronting Four Major Strategies of Satan

You can't stop birds from flying over your head', wrote Luther, 'but you can keep them from resting in your hair.' In this chapter, I want to give you a sampling of remedies that will assist you in following Luther's bold assertion.

Obviously, Satan's strategies and devices are too numerous to be covered in this small book. William Gurnall said quaintly that no actress has 'so many dresses to come in upon the stage with as the devil hath forms of temptation'. Instead, I will group some of his major devices under four major headings, then offer ways to refute each strategy. Many of the remedies suggested will also help you battle other satanic devices not listed here.

Strategy one: Satan entices us to sin

Device. Satan offers the bait of pleasure that hides the hook of sin. So Satan gave Adam and Eve a piece of fruit in exchange for Paradise. The hook of sin enveloped in the fruit led to punishment and death.

Remedies. (1) Remember the consequences of yielding to temptation. All sin is bittersweet. Sooner or later, Satan's snap trap will find you out. One evening my wife watched two mice carefully eat peanut butter from a snap trap. They were astonishingly clever; the trap never sprang. But two mornings later, those mice were dead in the trap. They had become more careless and bold.

Sin is a plague that inevitably incurs the saddest losses. 'All Satan's temptations are so many "welcome" notices [or billboards] along the broad road that leads to destruction', writes

J. I. Packer. 'Many eat that on earth which they digest in hell', Brooks says. William Gurnall put it this way: 'There is a spark of hell in every temptation.' These thoughts alone should keep us from playing with Satan's enticing bait.

(2) Don't toe-dangle. If you know you are weak in a certain area, stay away from situations where this temptation is likely to occur. For some, that may mean not going on the internet un-supervised and avoiding chat rooms. For others, it may mean cancelling catalogue browsing or trips to the mall, or keeping distance from bars and taverns. Know your own areas of weak-ness and flee them. Proverbs 5:8 says, 'Remove thy way from her, and come not nigh the door of her house.'

Do not ask how close you can come to sin without sinning, but strive to keep as far from sin as possible. 'If you don't want the devil to tempt you with forbidden fruit, you had better keep out of his orchard', Doug Barnett wrote. As Romans 12:9 says, 'Abhor that which is evil.' The Greek word for 'abhor' means to hate sin with horror, to hate it as hell itself.

(3) Stay actively involved in growth and ministry. David was especially vulnerable to temptation when he was not in the battle where he belonged (2 Sam. 11). Remember the old adage: 'Idle time is the devil's playground.'

(4) Share sustained temptations with a close, confidential, Christian friend. Since sin thrives in secrecy, bringing the issue out into the light helps to break its power by making you more accountable to handle it righteously (1 John 1:6-7). Pray with your friend and pray often on your own for spiritual strength to resist temptation (Matt. 26:41). Remember, lone rangers often become dead rangers. Christians need each other.

(5) Remember that you cannot remain neutral to any tempta-tion. Each temptation will drive you either closer to God or fur-ther away from him. 'Our response to temptation is an accurate barometer of our love for God', writes Erwin Lutzer.

Device. Satan presents sin as a virtue. He makes little of sin so as to retain the sinner. Pride becomes self-esteem, covetousness becomes ambition, and drunkenness becomes fellowship.

Remedy. Remember, sin is more dangerous when it is painted and disguised. But sin will eventually lose its covering and be exposed. We must see sin in all its blackness, the way we would see it on our deathbed. We must remember that the forgiveness of sin cost our Saviour his precious blood.

Device. Satan says repentance from sin is easy. By minimising the difficulty of repentance, Satan minimises the horrible nature of sin. That encourages us to keep on sinning.

Remedy. Repentance is so difficult that it is nearly impossible for us. 'Repentance is a flower that grows not in nature's garden', Thomas Brooks writes. True repentance is radical and comprehensive. As Brooks notes, 'to repent of sin is as great a work of grace as not to sin' (p. 63). Repentance is a daily, lifelong task that changes a whole person, moving the person continually from sin to God. It produces sorrow and shame for sin, confession, forsaking sin, and accepting sin's punishment. It makes a person loathe himself (Job 42:6; Ezek. 20:43) and fly to Christ alone for forgiveness and solace.

Device. Satan encourages us to make friends with worldly people. Satan knows that association begets assimilation, so he entices us to sin through friendships with ungodly people.

Remedy. Scripture warns us against the infectious danger of ungodly company. Ephesians 5:11 says, 'Have no fellowship with the unfruitful works of darkness, but rather reprove them.' Proverbs 5:14–16 says, 'Enter not into the path of the wicked, and go not in the way of evil men. Avoid it, pass not by it, turn from it, and pass away.'

Device. Satan presents unconverted people as people who have many outward mercies and few sorrows, and believers as having few outward mercies and many sorrows. In this way, Satan tries to convince us that it is vain to serve God (Ps. 73:1–15; Jer. 44:16–18).

Remedy. God's hand of mercy may seem to bless a person while God's heart condemns that person. That was the case with King Saul. Similarly, God's hand of mercy may seem to be against a person while his heart strongly loves that person. That was the case with Job. Many times God chastens those whom he loves (Heb. 12:5–6) for their eternal welfare. All afflictions, yes, 'all things work together for good to them that love God' (Rom. 8:28). In addition, the internal joys of believers are often greater than can be outwardly observed, whereas the internal needs of the wicked are always greater than their outward enjoyments.

Device. Satan minimises the seriousness of sin, then leads us on to greater sins. Sin encroaches upon us, moving from our thoughts to our looks to our words and then to our actions. Spurstowe says, 'Satan casts down none suddenly from the pinnacle of a high profession into the lowest abyss of wickedness, but leads them rather by oblique descents and turnings, lower and lower, until at last they take hold of hell' (p. 36).

Remedy. Brooks tells us that 'the least sin is contrary to the law of God, the nature of God, the being of God, and the glory of God'. Technically, there is no such thing as a little sin because there is no little God to sin against. Brooks sees committing a so-called 'little sin' as a great insult to God. 'The less the temptation is to sin, the greater is that sin', Brooks writes. 'So it is the greatest unkindness that can be showed to God, Christ, and the Spirit, for a soul to put God upon complaining, Christ upon bleeding, and the Spirit upon grieving, by yielding to little sins' (p. 41). When Satan tempts you to commit a little sin, tell him that you will not displease your greatest Friend who died for all your sin—including your smallest sins—by yielding to his greatest enemy.

A little sin can do great damage. Once you have begun to sin, you do not know how or where or when you will stop committing that sin. As Brooks writes, 'Little sins often slide into the soul, and breed, and work secretly and undiscernibly in the soul, till they come to be so strong, as to trample upon the soul, and to cut the throat of the soul' (p. 42). Ultimately, the smallest sin will bring the wrath of God down upon the one who commits it. Truly, Brooks was right in stressing that there is 'more evil in the least sin than in the greatest affliction' (p. 44).

Strategy two: Satan hinders spiritual disciplines

Device. Satan makes us focus on how difficult it is to practise spiritual disciplines. He discourages us from persevering in prayer, in Bible study, in fellowship with believers, and in holiness. He plants the thought that it's better for us to neglect these disciplines altogether than to undertake them in a perfunctory and unsatisfying manner.

Remedy. Counteract this satanic and self-defeating reasoning by focusing on God's command to use the spiritual disciplines. Read the Scriptures daily, diligently, systematically, and prayerfully. Regularly meditate on the truths of Scripture, for disciplined meditation will provide inner resources on which to draw (Ps. 77:10–12). Pray unceasingly, use the sacraments faithfully, regularly fellowship with believers, sanctify the Lord's Day, and witness to your neighbours.

Remember the benefits of spiritual disciplines. Practising spiritual disciplines may be hard at times, but the Holy Spirit will bless their use. Through prayer, Bible study, fellowshipping with believers, and other disciplines, we honour and enjoy God, meet and embrace Christ, kindle our love, establish our minds, and keep sin at bay. Our weak graces are strengthened, our languishing comforts are revived, our fears are scattered, and our hopes are raised. Practising the spiritual disciplines promotes godliness in every area of our lives.

Look more to the crown than the cross, more to future glory than present suffering. Remember that if you gain many benefits from the use of spiritual disciplines in this earthly wilderness, you will gain so much more in heaven. Heaven will more than make amends for all the work involved in maintaining spiritual disciplines.

Device. Satan afflicts our minds with vain thoughts to distract us from seeking God through spiritual disciplines. Such assaults can be so grievous and perplexing that we become weary of engaging in sacred duties.

Remedy. Focus on God's majestic holiness as you approach him. Confess your sin of indulging in wandering thoughts and tell God that you abhor those distractions. Then resist them through the Spirit's strength, and press on with the spiritual disciplines. Beg God for strength to set aside worldly cares. Ask him to increasingly fill you with heavenly and eternal truths. Strive for a large, growing, and varied acquaintance with God.

Focus on the spiritual disciplines rather than on the cares of this world. If your life is packed with secular obligations, trim back your obligations until you feel you have adequate time to seek God each day. Do not let business dealings intrude on your spiritual disciplines.

Martin Luther said that he wanted the devil to hear that he was serious about communing with God, so Luther practised his spiritual disciplines aloud. Speaking aloud aids concentration. For further help in battling distractions, read Richard Steele's *A Remedy for Wandering Thoughts*.

Strategy three: Satan misrepresents God and his truth
Device. Satan presents God as a harsh taskmaster. Ever since Genesis 3, Satan has portrayed God as hard and cold and distant. Satan has also slain multitudes of people by telling them that the holy, just, living God would not have mercy on them because they are too hard-hearted and sinful for God.

78

Remedy. Jonathan Edwards once preached a sermon on Psalm 25:11 ('For thy name's sake, O LORD, pardon mine iniquity; for it is great'), addressing this strategy of Satan. Edwards said we can understand David's cry for pardon only if we realize that David expected forgiveness solely because of God's name. David made the greatness of his own sins a ground to plead for forgiveness. Edwards concludes that just as a beggar begging for bread pleads the greatness of his poverty, so a man in spiritual distress calls for pity from God. No more 'suitable plea can be argued than the extremity of his case', Edwards says. The Triune God delights to receive beggars. He is not a harsh taskmaster who is unmoved by our poverty. Remember, as Charnock said, 'Satan paints God with his [Satan's] own colours.'

Device. Satan pushes the misconception that not all members of the Triune God are equally willing to save sinners. Satan doesn't mind sermons that make Christ sound willing to save sinners, if the preacher presents the Father and the Spirit as more reticent to save.

Remedy. Jesus truly 'receives sinners' with joy (Luke 15:2), but so does God the Father and God the Holy Spirit. God the Father so delights to save us that he gave his only-begotten Son to work out our salvation. God the Holy Spirit so delights to save us that he is willing to work with amazing patience in the hearts of all kinds of sinners.

Device. Satan sometimes stresses only the love and mercy of God. Satan convinces many people today not to be troubled about sin and their relationship with God, for God is full of mercy. Since God delights in mercy, and is always willing to show mercy, people don't need to be concerned about his justice, Satan says.

Remedy. God is indeed merciful, but his mercy is just. If mercy is used for a licence to sin, we sin against mercy. God will then 'rain hell out of heaven', as Thomas Brooks says, for 'sins against mercy will bring the greatest and sorest judgments upon men's heads and hearts'. Brooks goes on to say that God 'first hangs out the white flag of mercy', but if people reject his mercy, God will then 'put forth his red flag of justice and judgment' (pp. 51–52).

Believers must view the mercy of God as the most powerful argument to preserve them from sin, and not as an encouragement to sin (Ps. 26:3–5; Rom. 6:1–2). 'There is nothing in the world that renders a man more unlike to a saint, and more like to Satan, than to argue from mercy to sinful liberty; from divine goodness to licentiousness. This is devil's logic' (pp. 54–55).

Strategy four: Satan opposes sanctification

Device. Satan dampens obedience to the saving knowledge of gospel truth. Once you are saved and come under the refining process of God's pruning knife, Satan tries to bewilder you. Like Peter, you will then deny your Master and walk unworthy of the spiritual vocation to which you are called.

Remedy. Repent of your backslidings, return to God, and do the good works that you did so zealously in your time of first love (Rev. 2:4–5). Immerse yourself in the Scriptures and in solid biblical literature. Pray much to walk in firm, loving obedience before God.

Device. Satan stresses that intellectual knowledge of spiritual truth is enough. If other people who claim to be saved are satisfied just knowing about Christ, why should you long for more experiential knowledge of Christ? Satan doesn't mind if we continue to learn about Christ, but he works hard to prevent fact-gathering from turning into sanctified knowledge of the truth (2 Tim. 3:7). 'The devil does not care how many sermon pills you take so long as they do not work upon your conscience', wrote Thomas Watson.

Remedy: Settle for nothing less than Spirit-worked experiential knowledge of Christ (1 Cor. 1:30), and, by extension, knowledge of all the great truths of Scripture (2 Tim. 3:14–17). Christ, who is the living word (John 1:1) and the embodiment of truth, must be experientially known and embraced. As John 17:3 says, 'This is life eternal, that they might know thee, the only true God, and Jesus Christ, whom thou hast sent.' The word *know* in this text indicates a deep, abiding relationship.

Device. Satan makes sanctification look impractical because it is too difficult to understand. Satan tries to hide the beautiful simplicity of the way of holiness.

Remedy. Salvation and sanctification are free gifts. Remember, God, the great Giver of sanctification, lavishly works holiness in us, even when we fear it is only the size of a mustard seed. God also works within us the desire to give everything we are to him, not to earn our way into heaven, but because God's Spirit is prompting us in the way of holiness. This holy exchange is an uneven one, for Christ's gift of himself to us is far greater than our gift of ourselves to him. Yet this exchange is beautiful, simple, and mystical. It does not divorce itself from the Scriptures or the mind and work of the Holy Spirit. Trust God with childlike simplicity to sanctify you in Christ, for God has promised that Christ Jesus in us becomes our 'wisdom, righteousness, sanctification, and redemption' (1 Cor. 1:30).

Device. Satan makes us think that our salvation depends on our spiritual experiences, our holiness, or our works. He tries to confuse the true relationship between faith and works as well as gospel and law.

Remedy. A nineteenth-century believer rather quaintly explained his experience like this:

> I thought I must obey the law, and went to Moses to make terms with him, and he at once knocked me down. I knew I deserved it, and did not complain. I prepared

myself, and went again; and, with a severer blow, he brought me to the ground a second time. I was amazed, and entreated him to hear me. But he drove me from Sinai, and gave me no satisfaction. In my despair, I went to Calvary. There I found One who had pity on me, forgave my sins, and filled my heart with his love. I looked at him, and his healing mercy penetrated my whole being, and cured the malady within. Now, I went back to Moses to tell him what had happened. He smiled on me, shook my hand, and greeted me most lovingly; and he has never knocked me down since. I go by Calvary to Sinai, and all its thunders are silent (Wm. L. Parsons, *Satan's Devices and the Believer's Victory* [Boston, 1864], pp. 291–92).

Salvation is by grace alone. Do not trust any merits of your own. Take refuge daily by faith and repentance in Christ, the sinner's Saviour. Ask the Holy Spirit to continue to open your soul to God's love in Christ, and to prompt acts of grateful obedience that flow sweetly out of this fountain of love.

Device. Satan tries to dismiss what we do, saying that only what we believe is important. 'It is not so important to strive for higher levels of holiness in this life because there is only one thing needful and you have that', Satan says. 'You have been converted. You are on your way to heaven. When you die, you will be perfectly holy. Don't worry so much about being holy now.'

Remedy. Entertaining such a suggestion, even for a moment, is unworthy of a disciple of Christ. Scripture calls believers to grow in grace. It persuades us to leave those things that are behind and to press on toward greater spiritual maturity. It teaches us to be steadfast in obedience to Christ. Our usefulness and mission in the world oblige us to go forward, even though the sea and the wilderness are before us (Exod. 14:13–14). We must either overcome the world by faith or be overcome by it. If we fall back into unbelief, we will forget that we were 'purged from our old sins'

(2 Pet. 1:9). Our sins will then return sevenfold to pull us back into bondage.

Device. Satan says it is useless for us to try living in Christ while in this life. So few people truly overcome the world by faith, as John charges us to do (1 John 5:4), so why bother trying?

Remedy. Refuse to believe that defeat by the world, the flesh, and the devil is inevitable. Trust your Deliverer that he will make you a conqueror, by faith, through his own power. Fight the good fight of faith. By grace, claim the promises of Scripture as your own. Remember the covenant and oath of your Redeemer. Look to Christ for power to break the yoke of bondage and put you into 'the glorious liberty of the children of God' (Rom. 8:21).

Device. Satan entices us to be worldly by attacking us at our weakest points. He desensitises our consciences by encouraging us to compare ourselves with ourselves rather than with the standards set for us by Scripture.

Remedy. Remember, worldliness develops slowly in us. Like a malignant cancer, it is often not detected until it is too late. We must be circumspect. We must guard our hearts against worldliness. As John Flavel writes in *Keeping the Heart,* 'Set a watch before every gate that leads into or out of your heart.' We must set a guard at the gate of our imaginations, our minds, and our hearts. We must keep watch over our private thoughts. Like the psalmist, we must make sure that no wicked thing is set before our eyes.

One of the greatest dangers of worldliness today comes through our eyes. Every year, 4,000 evangelical pastors become enmeshed in internet pornography. Other people think nothing of spending numerous hours watching unedifying television shows or renting questionable movies to view at home.

Do not flirt with sin. Consider the man who lived at the top of a mountain. He needed to hire someone to take his daughter up and down the mountain each day for school. So he interviewed candidates, asking each one, 'How close can you come to the edge without going over?'

The first man said, 'I can come within twelve inches and not go over the edge.' The second said, 'I can come within six inches of the edge.' The third said he could come within an inch without falling over. But the fourth said, 'The closer I came to the edge, the more I'd be hugging the other side. So I choose to stay as far away from the edge as I can.' You know who got the job.

Stay away from worldliness. Recognise its danger before you go over the edge. Confess sin as soon as you are conscious of it. Keep a short account with God. Only a habitually clean conscience will grant us the unclouded, uninterrupted communion with God that we so desperately need. Sitting in heavenly places together with Christ Jesus (Eph. 2:6) is the best cure for daily struggles with worldliness.

Concluding advice

Donald Grey Barnhouse wrote, 'There is no need for ignorance concerning the devices of the devil, for they are set forth plainly in the Word of God, and they are also visible all around us.' And, we might add, they are exposed clearly in numerous books, particularly those written on the subject by able Puritans.

Space will not allow us to deal with other satanic strategies, such as how Satan keeps believers in doubt and darkness, capitalises on their inconsistencies, promotes division between believers and churches, fosters doctrinal error and apostasy, cultivates false spirituality, and promotes Satan-worship, demonism, and occultism.

Remedies for all these devices, however, usually follow similar patterns. Thomas Brooks, whose classic *Precious Remedies against Satan's Devices* has never been rivalled, summarised the Christian's duty in responding to Satan's devices in ten remedies. Brooks marshalled these remedies from the whole of Scripture:

1. Walk by the rule of Scripture
2. Don't vex or grieve the Holy Spirit
3. Pursue heavenly wisdom
4. Resist Satan's first overtures immediately
5. Strive to be filled with the Spirit
6. Remain humble
7. Maintain a strong and constant watch
8. Maintain communion with God
9. Fight Satan in Christ's strength, not your own
10. Pray much

Peter provides an even shorter summary. Let us obey his admonition: 'Be sober, be vigilant, because your adversary, the devil, as a roaring lion, walketh about, seeking whom he may devour; whom resist stedfast in the faith' (1 Pet. 5:8–9).

'Be sober': think clearly, think carefully, and, above all, think biblically.

'Be vigilant': be watchful; be alert to the signs of enemy presence, enemy activity, enemy purposes.

'Resist' the devil. His designs are always evil. The more you give him, the more he will want. Consider seriously what Brooks writes: 'Satan promises the best, but pays with the worst; he promises honour and pays with disgrace; he promises pleasure and pays with pain; he promises profit and pays with loss; he promises life and pays with death.'

Remain 'steadfast in the faith', unmoved, unyielding, using faith in God's Son and God's word as your shield. All shall then end well. By God's grace, you will be perfected, established, and strengthened. As Brooks concludes, 'Remember this, that your life is short, your duties many, your assistance great, and your reward sure; therefore faint not, hold on and hold up, in ways of well-doing, and heaven shall make amends for all.'

Finally, would you truly see Satan's defeat in your life? Focus on Christ. Remember who you are in Christ. Overcome the world by faith in Christ. Bear fruit for Christ's sake. Don't become a tempter for Christ's sake. Put all your hope in Christ. Trust his power. Love him and his people. Live in such a way that Christ means everything to you.

Part Four
Knowing Satan's Defeat
in Our Personal Lives, Churches, and Nations

Chapter 11

Our Challenge as Believers

Satan is like a condemned criminal on death row, living on borrowed time. Though still a roaring lion and an insidious tempter, he is mortally wounded. The world is subject to the Creator, not to the deceiver; to the Redeemer, not the enslaver. Frederick Leahy writes, 'Satan's counter-offensive is as hopeless as it is fierce. We must not believe his proud claim to the "kingdoms of the world"; his pretension to dominion is a lie. He is a usurper with no authority. It is God who holds the world in His hand, not this arch-pretender. And in God's world Satan is an imposter, a squatter with no rights' (*Satan Cast Out,* p. 31).

Christ defeated Satan at the cross and in the resurrection, but Satan still awaits final execution. Just as we who are believers live in what scholars call the *now/not yet* tension of the New Testament church (*now* we are saved but we are *not yet* what we will be in heaven when we are beyond the reach of Satan), so Satan lives in the New Testament era in a *now/not yet* tension—*now* he is defeated by Christ's death and resurrection, but he is *not yet* what he will be in hell, where he will be fully crushed and unable to even bruise the heel of the woman's seed.

From God's eternal perspective, the gap between the now and the not yet is virtually non-existent; from our perspective as time-bound creatures, we feel a gap between the two. One day when we are in heaven, that gap will appear only as a flickering moment. The gap is somewhat like the time between lightning and thunder. In reality, they happen at the same time, but because light travels faster than sound, we see the lightning first, then, seconds later, hear the thunder. In Christ's ministry, death, and

89

resurrection, Satan fell as lightning from heaven. On Judgement Day, we will hear the thunder of Satan's eternal destruction.

As believers living in the short space of time between the lightning and thunder, our responsibility is to tear down Satan's strongholds in our personal lives, in the church, and in our nation. In the power of Christ, our daily challenge is to deny Satan his goals, first, by living by faith; second, by bearing fruits; and third, by making the truths of Christ and his victorious gospel known to others. Let us now consider how, by God's grace, we can meet this challenge through the following resolutions:

1. *Resolve to live according to your identity in Christ.* That's Paul's profound imperative to believers throughout Romans 6. Paul summarises what he is saying in verse 11, 'Reckon ye also yourselves to be dead indeed unto sin, but alive unto God through Jesus Christ our Lord.' In verse 22, Paul says that as Christians we are freed from sin, and in verses 7 and 11, he explains that this is so because we have died to sin. Freedom from sin is grounded in our new identity as Christian believers. We cannot go on living in sin because, by definition, we have died to sin (v. 2).

    Paul appeals in verses 3–5 to our baptism. We have been baptised into Jesus Christ, which includes union with his death and resurrection. Those are the realities that dominate our new identity. As true believers, there is nothing more important for you and me to grasp when asking who we are than to see our ourselves as people who have died to sin in union with Jesus Christ and who have been raised to newness of life.

    Paul speaks about sin in Romans 5 and 6, not simply as deeds that we do, but as an oppressor who haunts our lives. In Romans 5:21 Paul implies that sin has reigned over us as a monarch unto death. He says, 'That as sin hath reigned unto death, even so might grace reign through righteousness unto eternal life by Jesus Christ our Lord.' Then in Romans 6:14, Paul says, 'For sin shall not have dominion over you: for ye are not under the law, but under grace.' In other words, sin rules over people like a tyrant. Verse 13 continues, 'Neither yield ye your members as instruments of unrighteousness unto sin.' Here Paul portrays sin as a kind of five-star general to whom individuals offer their bodies as weapons. Finally, in verse 23, Paul says, 'For the wages of sin is death; but the gift of God is eternal life through Jesus Christ our Lord.' Sin, by nature, is a monarch ruling over us (5:21), a tyrant beating us down (6:14), a general that wants to use our bodies as weapons (6:13), and an employer that pays us the wages of death at the end of the day (6:23).

In all these images, Paul paints sin as a lord and master ruling over us. He does not limit sin to deeds that we do or our failures to do right, but reveals it as a power that has gripped our lives, mastered us, and enslaved us. Paul is saying, 'Christian friends, all of us have been baptised into Christ, which means that we were also baptised into his death. Jesus suffered upon the cross, putting himself under the reign of sin. But he broke the power of sin in his death; he emerged victorious over sin. His holiness destroyed the powers that held him down and broke the chains of death that held him captive. In his resurrection, Christ overcame the dominion of sin and death and Satan. We who are united through grace to Jesus Christ also share in that victory over the dominion of sin. We have been set free from sin's authority. Sin need no longer grip our lives, master us, and enslave us.'

Paul is not saying that Christians will not continue to commit isolated sins. He is not saying that Christians are perfect and sinless, either. What he is saying is that every Christian believer who is united to Jesus Christ is free from the dominion, authority, rule, and kingdom of sin, because God has led believers out of the kingdom of darkness into the kingdom of his beloved Son. Paul is saying to Roman Christians and to us, 'Do not be confused about which kingdom you belong to; when you are tempted to sin, recognise that you belong to the kingdom of Christ. Have confidence in the cross where Satan was defeated, then tell sin and Satan to be gone. Tell them, "You are no longer masters over me; you no longer pay my wages, you are no longer my monarchs, and I am no longer slave to your tyranny. I belong to Christ; he is my sovereign. I have died to the dominion of sin and am free of its plagues. I will battle every movement of sin and the devil.'"

What Paul says is difficult for us to feel. I don't feel that I am free from sin. But there are times when you don't feel your nationality or your marital status, either. Nonetheless, these roles are fundamental realities of your life, and they have all kinds of implications for how you behave. Likewise, Paul says, 'Beloved, if we are married to Jesus Christ, and he has taken us through his death to newness of life, then that is the kind of person we are. Recognising that role will profoundly affect the way we live.'

Dear believer, regardless of what you feel, Paul says that you have died to the 'old man' of sin within you (v. 6). The 'old man' refers to your sinful nature, which you have through Adam's sin. Now that you have been united to Christ in his death and resurrection, the old man Adam no longer rules in you. Christ, the second Adam, has replaced the first Adam. Since you are no longer in Adam but in Christ, your life is no longer dominated by sin, shame, and guilt. The effects of the old Adam may still be in you but they no longer dominate your life. What now dominates your life is God causing you to grow as a new creation in Jesus Christ (2 Cor. 5:19). Your life as a Christian testifies that you are no longer dominated by what you were in Adam, but by what Jesus Christ has done for you. What Jesus has done for you increasingly permeates your being until one day you will be like him.

The point of Romans 6 is that we have no business yielding to Satan's temptations because he no longer is our head or our landlord. He is a defeated foe even for us because we are in Christ. That liberates us. Are you acquainted with

this liberation experientially? When the Emancipation Proc-
lamation was signed in 1863, freeing America's slaves, many
slaves failed to get the message right away. They still thought
and acted like slaves, and allowed themselves to be treated
like slaves. Paul is saying, as it were, 'Let us not be like that,
for, by God's grace, we are free men in Christ. When Satan
comes to tempt us to bring us back into the bondage of sin,
let's say to him, "Devil, you have come to the wrong address.
If you want me, you must go to my Head who is in heaven,
for I am in him. He is my new Landlord; I owe all my allegiance to him. Satan, you are no longer landlord of my life;
I no longer have to pay you rent. As for me, I am resolved to
live the life I was meant to live as a saved sinner made alive
in Christ."'

2. *Resolve to overcome the present, evil world by faith in Christ.*
First John 5:4b–5 says, "This is the victory that overcometh
the world, even our faith. Who is he that overcometh the
world, but he that believeth that Jesus is the Son of God?'
By 'overcoming the world', John does not mean conquering the people of this world, winning power battles over
our colleagues, or dominating others. Nor does John mean
withdrawing from the world, such as monks or Amish people
tend to do in establishing their own communities. A Christian
is called to fight *in* this world even though he is not *of* this
world. To escape from the world is like a soldier avoiding
injury by running from the battlefield. Escaping is not overcoming.

Overcoming also doesn't mean sanctifying everything
in the world for Christ. Some parts of the world may be redeemed for Christ, but sinful activities can never be sanctified. For John, overcoming means fighting by faith against
the flow of this present, evil world. It means rising above
this world's thinking and customs. It means persevering in
freedom in Christ apart from worldly enslavement. It means

striving for allegiance to God rather than the world. It means finding freedom only in Christ and his service, so that we sing with the psalmist:

> *I am, O Lord, Thy servant, bound yet free,*
> *Thy handmaid's son, whose shackles Thou hast broken;*
> *Redeemed by grace, I'll render as a token*
> *Of gratitude my constant praise to Thee.*

> --Psalter 426, stanza 9 (Psalm 116)

It means being raised above the circumstances of this world, so that, like Paul, we learn to be content in whatever state we find ourselves, knowing that all things work together for good to those that love God (Rom. 8:28). It means anchoring our lives in Christ and eternal things rather than this world and temporal things—living, for Christ's sake, above the threats and bribes and jokes of the world. It means following the Lord like Caleb (Num. 14:24) in the midst of complainers. It means remaining at peace when friends or people at work despise us for serving the Lord.

Overcoming the world by faith means living a life of self-denial. When God called Abraham to leave his family and friends in Haran, Abraham obeyed, not knowing where he was going. When the well-watered plain of Jordan lay before him, he didn't ask to move there, as his nephew Lot did. When God asked him to sacrifice his son, Isaac, through whom all the promises of the covenant would come, Abraham unsheathed his knife and prepared to kill his son in obedience to God. A life of self-denial often means that we have to die many deaths now, as we serve God in this world.

Overcoming the world by faith means patiently enduring all the persecutions the world throws at us. Spurgeon advised: 'Overcome the world by patiently enduring all the persecution that falls to your lot. Do not get angry; and do not become downhearted. Jests break no bones; and if you had any bone broken for Christ's sake, it would be the most honoured bone in your whole body.'

A dear colleague from South Africa told me of some of his arrests in Sudan. He said he experienced only 'minor persecution', such as having his head submerged in a pail of urine until he was forced to drink it, or having a bag tied around his head at the neck until he fainted from lack of oxygen. 'That's nothing compared to what our Lord experienced', he quickly added. 'We Christians must count it all joy when we are persecuted for Christ's sake.'

Most of us will not suffer such persecution, but if we are to overcome the world, we must not be friends of this world. As John tells us, worldly people who hated Christ will also hate his disciples. As 1 Timothy 3:12 says, 'All that will live godly in Christ Jesus shall suffer persecution.' It is far better to have the devil and worldly people as your adversaries than as your friends. Remember that a world that smiles upon you is a dangerous place.

3. *Resolve to resist the devil by fighting under the banner of Christ.* James 4:7 says, 'Resist the devil and he will flee from you.' Resist means to withstand, to set oneself against something. We are always to be against Satan, opposing him at every point. We must oppose him with our will, our thought, our conscience, our heart, our might, and our strength. We must remain firm in our faith, holding consistently to the word of God. We must allow no concessions to the devil.

We must oppose Satan by firmly resolving to do so. By God's grace we must resolve to yield to no assault of Satan, to succumb to no affliction. Resolve is half the battle. To resolve for God is to rout Satan. Hesitation loses resolve and welcomes Satan into your home. Lingering yields to Satan's devices. Yielding an inch to him is an invitation for him to take all. Satan cannot tolerate firm, decisive opposition.

We must fight, overcome, and defeat the devil, using the same weapon to defeat him that Jesus used—the word of

God. Only God's word will make the devil flee from you.

John said, 'He that is begotten of God keepeth himself, and that wicked one toucheth him not' (1 John 5:18). 'Keeping ourselves' by God's gracious strength is the surest pledge that Satan will not keep us. You keep yourself by resting on the Bible, the written word, and on Christ Jesus, the living Word. Satan cannot gain the victory over Scripture when it is rightly used, nor over Christ and his blood. Every view of Calvary makes Satan retreat. Christ's wounds are mightier than Satan's greatest strength. As one divine said of the devil, 'He turns pale at every view of Calvary.'

A heart sprinkled with Christ's blood is holy ground upon which Satan fears to tread. Experiencing salvation through that atoning blood is infallible protection against Satan. Scripture tells us that those in heaven have overcome Satan 'by the blood of the Lamb and the word of our testimony' (Rev. 12:11).

4. *Resolve to bear fruit for Christ's sake.* Jesus said, 'By their fruits ye shall know them', meaning that believers are recognised by certain attitudes and actions. Jesus tells us in John 15 that genuine fruit only comes from being united with Christ and abiding in him (v. 4). Whatever gifts or virtues you have, you cannot bear fruit apart from Christ. If you would bear fruit, get close to the true Vine, then trust Christ's energy in you to produce fruit. Forsake every sin that distracts you from abiding in Christ and saps your energy.

Philippians 1:11 says that God produces the fruits of righteousness in us so that he may be glorified. The fruits of righteousness include fruits of attitude and fruits of action. The fruits of attitude, according to Galatians 5:22–23, are love, joy, peace, longsuffering, gentleness, goodness, faith, meekness, and temperance. These are not natural characteristics in us. Rather, they are spiritual characteristics of our Saviour; they flow to us from the Spirit's saving work. If the fruits of attitude are in our lives, the fruits of action will follow.

Note that the fruits of attitude do not develop individually but as a package. Paul speaks of 'fruit' in the singular sense. We don't move from love to joy to peace; rather, the Holy Spirit works all of these fruits together in our lives as we abide in Christ.

The fruits of action also serve as offerings to God. Hebrews 13:15 describes a life of thankful praise: 'By him [Christ] therefore let us offer the sacrifice of praise to God continually, that is, the fruit of our lips giving thanks to his name.' Romans 15:28 speaks of helping those who are in need. Paul says that he would seal to the Gentiles 'the fruit' given by the Romans. If a gift is offered to someone in need from a loving heart flowing out of the divine energy of the indwelling Christ, that is a fruit of action. So Paul says, 'God loveth a cheerful giver' (2 Cor. 9:8). Colossians 1:10 refers to pure conduct as a fruit of action: 'That ye might walk worthy of the Lord unto all pleasing, being fruitful in every good work.'

Satan is powerless when a Christian's life reveals true fruit. Even ungodly people are struck by godly attitudes and actions. The way you live either builds up God's kingdom or Satan's kingdom. A backsliding Christian can do much damage. A fruit-bearing, godly Christian can do much good.

Recently, a survey was taken of several thousand church attendees. In answer to the question, 'What drew you to attend church the first time?' more than 90 per cent said they were attracted to church by the godly attitude or action of an individual member of that church. If you profess Christianity, never forget that the world is watching you closely.

Fruit-bearing is rooted in the Holy Spirit's saving work in our souls, which, in turn, arouses in our minds a present-tense, total commitment to God. It then works outward in our words and actions through all of life (Phil. 2:12-13). It influences everything we are, do, think, speak, or plan. It impacts our loving, our hating, our silences, our sorrowing, and our rejoicing. It is inseparable from our recreation, our business, our friendships, and our relationships.

Fruit-bearing is a daily task. It involves our entire soul and our entire body. Fruit-bearing is biblical piety put into action. John Calvin said our entire life 'must be an exercise in piety'. Exercising true piety is a lifetime commitment to live 'through Christ to God-ward' (2 Cor. 3:4), to win our neighbours for Christ, and to break down the kingdom of Satan.

Are you cultivating the fruits of the Spirit in your life in gratitude to God and in dependence upon his Spirit? Do you diligently use the spiritual disciplines for this purpose? Are you genuinely concerned that every part of your life will show the fruit of holiness so that others will want to have what you have? Do your talk and walk, your attitudes and actions, align with Scripture? Do your family and friends recognise that, despite your shortcomings, you are a sincere, fruit-bearing Christian?

5. *Resolve not to be a tool of the tempter.* Satan tempts us directly by speaking to our minds and working on our emotions, and he tempts us indirectly through another person such as a family member, friend, work associate, or stranger. The other person is usually an unbeliever, but as Paul tells us in Romans 14, that person can also be a believer who becomes a tool of Satan.

The motivation for tempting someone to sin may be to gratify the flesh. A person has some need or desire, and tempts someone else to help him satisfy it. Or a person wants to ease his own guilt by getting someone else involved in a sin. Whatever the motivation, Christians become most like the devil when they allow themselves to tempt others to sin.

Jesus pronounces a divine curse upon those who tempt others to sin. He says in Matthew 18:6–7, 'But whoso shall offend one of these little ones which believe in me, it were better for him that a millstone were hanged about his neck, and that he were drowned in the depth of the sea. Woe unto the world because of offences! for it must needs be that offences come; but woe to that man by whom the offence cometh!'

Earlier in Matthew 18, Jesus had just talked about how precious little children are, specifically young children in grace, or new converts. By extension, of course, all believers are children in their relationship to Christ. So Jesus is warning any believer or unbeliever about the seriousness of tempting a child of God to sin. He is saying that we then do what Satan does, and must expect to suffer the consequences of that act.

A millstone was used in Jesus' day to grind wheat into flour. The stone was about eighteen inches in diameter, and three or four inches thick. It had a hole in the centre and a handle on the side. This thick stone would be placed on top of another stone. Women would then turn the handle or stick as they poured grain through the little hole to produce flour for their bread.

Another kind of grinding wheel was up to five feet in diameter and several feet thick. This wheel was so heavy that it had to be pulled by a donkey. Stone rolled upon stone, grinding away at the grain. Whether Jesus meant the smaller or larger stone isn't important. The point is that a person who wilfully tempts a believer to sin would be better off having a rope attached to a millstone tied around his neck, then thrown in the sea to drown. The tempter would be better off dead than alive.

Jesus was justifiably extreme in his pronouncement against leading a believer astray. It is bad enough to person- ally sin against God and to bear the penalty for that sin, but in tempting someone else to sin, the tempter becomes the propa- gator and catalyst of sin. Such a tempter is a danger to every believer. Just as a terrorist is a danger to our physical welfare, so a person who works for Satan is a danger to our spiritual welfare. God says that a tempter is better off dead than inciting others to fall into sin and wreck their lives.

Jesus goes on to say in verse 7, 'Woe unto the world because of offences! for it must needs be that offences come; but woe to that man by whom the offence cometh!' The word *woe* warns of coming destruction. In Matthew 23, Jesus used that word seven times, pronouncing punishment by saying, 'Woe unto you, scribes and Pharisees.' In Matthew 26, Jesus pronounced woe upon Judas Iscariot, who would betray Christ. Enticements to sin are inevitable, Jesus says, but woe to that person through whom temptation comes.

The woes of Jesus continue today. Woe to the husband who shows no love to his wife, thereby teaching his newly married son not to realise the importance of loving his young bride. Woe to the wife who fails to submit to her husband, showing her newly married daughter that it isn't important to support her young bridegroom as head of the family. Woe to the young man who takes a job to support his family by becoming a bartender, but whose actions entice others to sin through alcohol. Woe to the young lady who dresses seductively and raises sinful thoughts in a God-fearing young man.

You might object that you know people who tempt others to fall, but you don't see them suffering any 'woes'. They are getting along just fine. My friend, the only thing you know about someone else is what you see and hear. You often do not know what people are feeling. You do not know their struggles with pain and suffering. You do not know how tempting others to sin has wrecked their lives and families, divided their children, and caused their businesses to collapse. You do not know how the weight of that sin has burdened their hearts and obsessed their thoughts. You do not know whether they are getting along well or not.

The bottom line is this: do not in any way act as a tool of Satan by tempting someone to sin. You will pay dearly for it. Pray daily that you will never injure the name of your Saviour. Beg forgiveness of God for any way in which you have unintentionally influenced others to stumble in their walk with God.

Chapter 12

Our Challenge as Church Members

Our challenge to live as the church of Jesus Christ in the wake of Satan's defeat involves making the following commitment:

1. *Resolve to live by Scripture alone. Sola scriptura* was the battle cry of the Reformation. The Reformers taught that Scripture is perfect, complete, clear, authoritative, inerrant, and fully inspired by the Holy Spirit from the first chapter of Genesis to the last chapter of Revelation. To defeat Satan in the church, do not expect the church to be perfect. Rather, help the church work for perfection by reforming her according to the Scriptures. Scripture is the hub out of which radiates law and gospel, doctrine and preaching, guidance and authority. Defeat Satan by striving to make Scripture the pre-eminent touchstone and infallible norm in the church.

   Affirming the infallibility, inerrancy, and authority of Scripture is not enough for the church. She must also be freed from office-bearers within her that twist her teachings to allow a demythologized Bible, women in office, and gay marriages. She needs to experience Scripture as God speaking to us as a father speaks to his children. God gives us his word as truth and power. When the church is scriptural in its profession, teaching, spiritual experience, and living, the gospel is 'the power of God (*dunamis,* or dynamite) unto salvation' (Rom. 1:16).

   The word of God is the church's most powerful weapon against Satan and his kingdom. As Luther wrote, 'All those stones that the Davids of God have flung at the Goliaths [of Satan] have been taken out of the brook of Scriptures.' Satan fears no weapon more than the sword of the Spirit, the word of God. The church today urgently needs to demonstrate the transforming power of God's word. That power must be evident in the way church members live in their homes, schools, businesses, community, and market place. Church members must sincerely and humbly show that though other books may inform or even reform them, only one book can transform them and make them conform to the image of Christ. Only as 'living epistles of Christ' (2 Cor. 3:3) can we hope to win the battle for the Bible in our day. If only half the strength we spend attacking or defending the Bible was devoted to knowing and living the Scriptures, how many more people would fall under Scripture's transforming power!

Today's church must become more word-centred in preaching, praying, worshiping, and living. As Henry Smith says: 'We should set the Word of God always before us like a rule, and believe nothing but that which it teacheth, love nothing but that which it prescribeth, hate nothing but that which it forbiddeth, do nothing but that which it commandeth' (*Works,* 1:494). When the word becomes central in our churches, Satan will be defeated. We will experience what John Flavel says: 'The Scriptures teach us the best way of living, the noblest way of suffering, and the most comfortable way of dying.'

Do you personally know, love, and live Holy Scripture? Do you search God's word and relish it? Can you say with Ezekiel, 'It was in my mouth as honey for sweetness' (Ezek. 3:3)? Is the Bible your first love or do you spend more time reading the newspaper or surfing the internet? Is Scripture our mirror for dressing (James 1), our rule for working (Gal. 6:16), our water for washing (Ps. 119:9), our food for nourishment (Job 23:12), our sword for fighting (Eph. 6:17), our counsellor for resolving doubts and fears (Ps. 119:24), and our heritage for enrichment (Ps. 119:111)? Are our consciences, like Luther's, captive to the word of God?

2. *Resolve to live by saving faith in, and hard work under, Christ's lordship.* Faith in the lordship of Christ is the backbone of the church's service. It never forgets the church is at war; it provides peace in the midst of spiritual conflict. The true Christian is in Christ, and belonging to Christ empowers us to triumph over Satan and all his forces. In Christ, the church is safe no matter how dark the times. God's people are optimists because their Saviour is victorious. He is the lion of the tribe of Judah. He is the Mighty God born in a manger at Bethlehem. He goes forth now until the last day, conquering and to conquer. He says to his church, 'Ye believe in God, believe also in me' (John 14:1), and the church responds with Paul in 2 Corinthians 2:14, 'Thanks be unto God who always causeth us to triumph in Christ.'

When the church is passionately convinced that Christ is Lord, and that conviction is wedded to a deep love of the Saviour and daily communion with him, the church's future is truly bright. She knows that Christ is mightier than Satan and that all the demons of hell cannot pluck her from the Father's hand.

We can then entrust the church to Christ's hands, knowing that the church belongs to him. Christ promises, 'I *will* build *my* church' (Matt. 16:18). His lordship will prevail. That's why Luther could say before going to sleep: 'Lord Jesus Christ, I now need rest, so I lift the burdens of the church off my shoulders and put them on Thine. I will rest in peace knowing that Thou art the keeper of the church. In the morning, I'll get back in harness again.' Luther had faith in Christ's lordship over his church. The church is God's worksite where God brings great faith and hard work together.

Jesus Christ is the mediator, minister, surety, and lord of his church. The substance with which he builds his church is sinners. He changes sinners by his power, makes them confessors of his name, and works commitment in their lives. The gates of hell will not prevail against the church of God (Matt. 16:18). Throughout history, even when the church seemed overwhelmed by the powers of darkness, she has survived and grown. 'God in the midst of her doth dwell.' John Flavel said to people who were quick to mourn a faltering church, 'Be not too quick to bury the church before she be dead.'

The church may stagger, but she will surely continue her march through history to ultimate triumph. That is because Jesus Christ guarantees her success as Lord. He will never dismiss her as irrelevant, as others do. Individual churches may close their doors, denominations may wither, but the church of Christ will grow and prosper. As the Belgic Confession (Art. 27) says, 'This holy church is preserved or supported by God against the rage of the whole world, even though she sometimes (for a while) appears very small and in the eyes of men—to be reduced to nothing: as during the perilous reign of Ahab the Lord reserved unto Him seven thousand men who had not bowed their knees to Baal.'

If we truly grasped God's perspective of the church, many of the problems we struggle with in the local church would seem small. Consider this, for example. While Israel saw only the rubbish of Jerusalem, God saw rebuilt walls (Isa. 49:16). When we see a church torn by dissension, God sees a glorious church elected by the Father (Eph. 1:3–6), redeemed by the Son (Eph. 1:7), and adopted by the Spirit (Rom. 8:15). She is glorious because of her role in the plan of God (Eph. 3:10–11), her holiness (Eph. 2:10), her access to God (Heb. 4:16), and her distinguished inheritance (Eph. 1:14, 18). As John Newton wrote:

> *Glorious things of thee are spoken,*
> *Zion, city of our God,*
> *He whose word cannot be broken*
> *formed thee for his own abode:*
> *On the Rock of Ages founded,*
> *what can shake thy sure repose?*

With salvation's walls surrounded,
thou may'st smile at all thy foes.

True Christians are members of the only long-standing, successful institution on earth. 'No group, no movement, no institution of any kind in the world can even approach to the glory, the splendour, the honour, the beauty, the magnificence, the wonder, the dignity, the excellence, the resplendency of the church of God', wrote Daniel Wray (*The Importance of the Local Church,* pp. 4–7). We should serve the church, and Christ through the church, with all our hearts, always remembering that our labour is not in vain in the Lord (1 Cor. 15:58).

The church is a fleet of fishing boats, not a yacht club; it is a hospital for sinners, not a museum for saints. We dedicate our lives to a work in progress: to what Christ has promised and paid for with his own blood. We work for that which is worthwhile and shall be successful in the end, though there will always be dross amid the gold. The church's work, therefore, is never in vain. It is the product of God's sovereign grace in Christ, not the product of the mind and efforts of men.

Christ's promise that he will build the church is already being fulfilled. But this side of the Day of Judgement, the church is under construction. And like any building site, this place of construction isn't necessarily tidy or impressive. It includes piles of bricks and boards, ugly trenches, waste, rubble, and abandoned tools.

If we look at that mess, we can easily become discouraged. We see so many unfinished people in the church who are full of imperfections and weakness. If we think we are going to find something better than that, we only set up ourselves for disappointment. Instead of criticising people who fall short of our expectations, however, we ought to put on our boots, overalls, and helmets, and get busy on the worksite.

We should also prepare ourselves for a lot of hard work that may not seem to get much accomplished. *Ora et labora* ('pray and work!') must become our work song. 'The church of Christ needs servants of all kinds, and instruments of every sort; penknives as well as swords, axes as well as hammers, Marthas as well as Marys, Peters as well as Johns', wrote J.C. Ryle. Though we will struggle with many challenges in church work, we must press on, always remembering what the church is going to be some day—a bride adorned for her husband, without spot or wrinkle. 'The church shall survive the world, and be in bliss when that is in ruins', wrote Matthew Henry. 'When men are projecting the church's ruin, God is preparing for its salvation.'

If Christ shall get the victory over Satan by the word, and if he commissions his church to preach the word all over the world to accomplish his purposes, the church's privilege is to love one another, obey her Lord's mandate, and leave the outcome in his sovereign hand. The church must rest—also in days like Noah's—in the assurance that God's word will not return to him void (Isa. 55:11). We work confidently, not feverishly, knowing that the Harvester is God and the harvest is in his hands. When we forget this, we doubt, fear, and panic; but when we act upon this and bring the gospel to the ends of the earth, we rejoice in the obedience of faith and believe that Satan shall be bruised under our feet shortly.

3. *Resolve to live for reformation and revival in the church.* To keep Satan at bay, the church must continue striving for reformation. She must recover what she has lost since the great Protestant Reformation. The sixteenth-century Reformers fought on four major fronts. The first area was reforming worship. Calvin regarded worship as the fundamental battleground, since the church comes to its fullest expression in worship. Oh, how we need to return today to simple, biblical, reformation worship in Spirit and truth that centres on the unadulterated preaching of the whole counsel of God's

word—death in Adam and life in Christ! Too many churches attract people to their services through gimmicks without realising that whatever gimmick a church does to get people inside must be continued to keep people there. Surely Satan has no trouble with churches that depart from word-centred, Christ-centred worship. He is not fighting such churches, but as Vance Havner says, 'he is joining them. He does more harm by sowing tares than by pulling up wheat. He accomplishes more by imitation than by outright opposition.'

The second front of the Reformation was the doctrinal concern to recover biblical views of God, man, salvation, the work of the Spirit, and the sacraments. The church of today needs to return to the basic hallmarks of the Reformation: the basic *solas,* the five points of Calvinism, the covenant of grace, the lordship of Christ, the saving work of the Spirit, and the transcendent sovereignty of God.

The third front of the Reformation was church polity and discipline. Here are its basic principles: the Lord Jesus Christ is sole Head of the church (Col. 1:18). He has established government in the church (Matt. 16:19), which he entrusts to office-bearers (Eph. 4:11-12), who must exercise scriptural, spiritual power and discipline (John 18:36; Matt. 28:19-20) for the well-being of the church (Tit. 1:5). That discipline must be preventative and corrective. Calvin called discipline the third mark of the true church. He believed that if the key of church discipline became rusty through disuse, the other two marks of the church—pure preaching and the right administration of the sacraments—would also lose their cutting edge as a helpful medicine. Today, most churches do not use the key of discipline or use it crassly, without love. Even those that do use it, usually discipline too late. And when they do, they meet stiff resistance from relatives or friends of the brother or sister who is being lovingly disciplined.

Finally, the Reformers fought for piety based on sound doctrine. For the Reformers, theological understanding and practical piety were inseparable. Calvin developed a comprehensive form of piety (*pietas*), which he claimed was the primary reason he wrote his *Institutes*. As I have shown elsewhere (*The Cambridge Companion to John Calvin,* ed. Donald K. McKim, pp. 125-52), Calvin's piety is evident in *practical practices* such as prayer, repentance, self-denial, cross-bearing, and obedience. It is evident in *theological doctrines* such as union with Christ, justification, and sanctification. But piety also is evident in *ecclesiastical matters.* Calvin spoke often of piety in the church, piety of the preached word through the internal minister (the Holy Spirit) by means of the external minister (the preacher). He spoke of piety in the law, piety in the sacraments, and piety in the psalter. The call to return to a comprehensive biblical piety is the most forgotten and neglected dimension of the Reformation.

The Reformers passionately believed that reformation was needed on these four fronts. They were not pragmatists who simply went with the flow as long as things worked. Rather, they reformed the church from its foundations up, building on the principles of biblical worship, sound theology, faithful polity, and comprehensive piety.

The church today must likewise strive to be a reforming church. It must not try to be what it thinks people want it to be. If we want the church to change the world, the church must first be put right. She must be what she is called to be in Scripture—a people set apart to worship the Lord in Spirit and in truth and to work for his kingdom in the earth.

The church also needs revival. Too often people who want to reform the church are unaware of the church's need for revival. But without revival, reformation in the church will remain cold and formal, and can even be destructive. When every pin in the tabernacle is brought under the scrutiny of reform-minded people whose hearts are not renewed and aflame with love for God, reformation will produce sterility, formality, legality, and perhaps church splits. Reformation without revival can turn ugly and brutal.

Revivals are 'times of refreshing [that] come from the presence of the Lord', Acts. 3:19 tells us. During revival, the Holy Spirit is poured out on sinners in an extraordinary way. Authentic revivals don't produce a different kind of Christianity; they breathe new life into true Christianity. They are not totally different from the regular experience of the church; the difference is a matter of degree. In a true 'outpouring of the Spirit', great numbers of people are born again. God's people grow in spiritual maturity in greater measure than usual. Spiritual influence becomes more widespread, conviction of sin goes deeper, and feelings are more intense. The sense of God's presence becomes more evident and love for God and others increase. Revival heightens all these marks of Christianity (Murray, *Revival and Revivalism,* p. 23).

As reformation needs revival, revival also needs reformation. Without constant reforming, revivals can be pulled off track by unscriptural abuses, bizarre phenomena, and spurious conversions. In revivals, chaff grows alongside good wheat, but the chaff begins to take over when revival is not coupled with reformation. Revivals are influenced by man, hence a winnowing season usually follows revival (Murray, pp. 82–85).

Authentic revivals vary immensely, but from the New Testament revivals recorded in the book of Acts to the great revivals in church history, such as the sixteenth-century Reformation, the Great Awakening of the 1740s, or the international revivals in the late 1850s, the marks of a true revival include the following:

a. The sovereign work of the Holy Spirit. The existence, depth, timing, and numbers of true revival are determined by God (Acts 2:47; 13:48).

b. A remarkable outpouring of prayer (Acts 1:14; 2:1).

c. A movement that begins in the church. True revival usually begins in the church with the reawakening and enlightening of those who have already been born again (Acts 2:2–4).

d.   Biblical preaching. Scripturally based preaching figures prominently in revival. Twelve of the twenty-two verses of Peter's Pentecost sermon that prompted revival are quotations from the Psalms and the prophets.

e.   Repentance. Revival is honest with the souls of people; its call to repentance is coupled with the rediscovery of truth (Acts 2:38). Reformation and revival go together.

f.   Faith. In true revival, the power of faith joins with the power of truth and repentance (Acts 2:39).

g.   Christ-centredness. Revival is always Christ-centred in an experiential manner.

h.   Evangelising (or 'gospelising'). When the church is revived, she spreads the gospel everywhere (Acts 13:48-49).

i.   Love. Revival prompts great love for the glory of God and the souls of others.

Revival without reformation promotes heat without light, zeal without soundness. To defeat Satan in our churches, we must pray for both reformation and revival. Pray for a 'reformational revival' and a 'revival reformation'. In the meantime, ask yourself if you truly yearn for reformation and revival. Do you strive to live in genuine piety in Christ? Do you walk worthy of the vocation to which you are called as a member of the body of Christ? Is that reflected in your private devotions and in your family worship? Does it then spill out into faithful use of the means of grace? Do you attend worship services, prayer meetings, and other ministries at church with prayerful zeal and wholehearted expectation? Do you expect great things from a great God? When there are no apparent conversions for many weeks, do you, like George Whitefield, ask with prayerful concern, 'Lord, what's wrong?'

4. *Resolve to live in oneness before Christ.* A parishioner called me one day, quite upset. She had been on a plane, next to a man who was praying. When he finished, she asked warmly, 'So you're a Christian?'

'No', he replied briskly.

'I thought you were praying', she persisted.

'I was', he said.

After a few minutes my parishioner asked, 'Sir, may I ask, to whom were you praying?'

He paused, then said, 'I was praying to Satan.'

'Why on earth would you pray to Satan?' she asked in amazement.

He responded, 'I was praying that Satan would be successful in severing the relationship between at least thirty pastors and their congregations in North America this week.'

My parishioner was dumbfounded. 'The man looked so sincere as he prayed', she said to me. 'He seemed more earnest than I am in most of my prayers.'

Satan delights in divisiveness. He delights in rending the body of Christ. To counteract Satan, the church must strive to realise her unity in Christ. We must strive for good communication and understanding. We must defy Satan's attempts to split the church.

The Nicene Creed confesses 'one church' (*unam ecclesiam*), meaning the church is built upon one rock, one Messiah, one confession. The Westminster Confession says that the church's unity lies in Jesus Christ: 'The catholic or universal church, which is invisible, consists of the whole number of the elect, that have been, are, or shall be gathered into one, under Christ the Head thereof; and is the spouse, the body, the fullness of him that filleth all in all' (Chapter 25.1). That the church is Christ's body and he the head (Col. 1:18) implies that Christ and the church are complementary, for a body and a head cannot exist without each other.

Wilhelmus à Brakel said the church and Christ are each other's property. Their union is affirmed by the gift of Christ to the church, Christ's purchase of and victory for the church, the indwelling of Christ's Spirit within the church, and the church's surrender by faith and love to Christ (*The Christian's Reasonable Service*, 2:87–90). To think of Christ without the church severs what God has wedded together in holy union.

The church is organically related to Christ more profoundly than any organic relationship that falls within the realm of our experience; she is rooted and built up in Christ (Col. 2:7), clothed with Christ (Rom. 13:14), and cannot live without Christ (Phil. 1:21). 'The church is in Christ as Eve was in Adam', wrote Richard Hooker.

All the members of Christ's body are united to one another because of their common Head (1 Cor. 12). All true believers who confess Christ as their exclusive Saviour are 'joined and united with heart and will, by the power of faith, in one and the same Spirit', says the Belgic Confession in Article 27. They are united as members of the household of God, the community of Christ, and the fellowship of the Spirit. There is one gospel (Acts 4:12), one revelation (1 Cor. 2:6–10), one baptism (Eph. 4:5), and one Lord's Supper (1 Cor. 10:17).

A. A. Hodge said that if there is one God, one Christ, one Spirit, and one cross, there can only be one church (*Confession of Faith,* pp. 310ff.). The believers of this one church are described in New Testament images such as salt of the earth, the holy temple, the new creation, sanctified slaves, sons of God, and fighters against Satan. They are many branches in one vine, many sheep in one flock, and many stones in one building. The church is 'a chosen generation, a royal priesthood, an holy nation, a peculiar people; that ye should show forth the praises of him who hath called you out of darkness into his marvellous light' (1 Pet. 2:9).

The church's oneness in Christ is indestructible, for it

comes from Christ. Her unity can be disrupted, however. When it is, we should feel shame and grief at how divided the church can become because of her unfaithfulness to Christ and her deviation from the apostolic pattern of unity. Sins such as inattention to doctrinal and practical purity (1 Tim. 6:11–21), autonomy (1 Cor. 1:10–17), factionalism (1 Cor. 3:1–23), lust for power (3 John 9), unwillingness to seek reconciliation (Matt. 5:23–26), failure to maintain church discipline (Matt. 18:15–20), and unwillingness to help needy believers (Matt. 25:31–46) tear apart the body of Christ.

Still, even the multiplicity of church splits caused by rifts between believers cannot divide the true family of Christ. Brothers and sisters in a family may quarrel and separate, but they still remain members of one family. Likewise, the church is one body in Christ with many members (Rom. 12:3–8; 1 Cor. 12:27), one family of God the Father (Eph. 4:6), and one fellowship in the Spirit (Acts 4:32; Eph. 4:31–32). As Paul wrote to the Ephesians, 'There is one body, and one Spirit, even as ye are called in one hope of your calling; one Lord, one faith, one baptism, one God and Father of all, who is above all, and through all, and in you all' (4:4–6).

Rightly understood, the church's oneness helps us avoid the kind of unity that is had at the expense of her confessions of truth. Some divisions are essential to keep the true church separate from the false. 'Division is better than agreement in evil', George Hutcheson said. Those who support spurious unity by tolerating error and heresy forget that a split based on biblical essentials helps to preserve the true unity of the body of Christ. 'The devil's war is better than the devil's peace', remarked Samuel Rutherford.

The church's oneness helps us avoid splits over nonessential doctrines as well as egotistical differences. Such splits violate the unity of the body of Christ. As Samuel Rutherford warned, 'It is a fearful sin to make a rent and a hole in Christ's mystical body because there is a spot in it.' Such disunity offends the Father who longs to see his family living in harmony; it offends the Son who died to break down walls of hostility; and it offends the Spirit who dwells within believers to help them live in unity.

Church members must realise that they cannot touch any part of the church's body without affecting the whole body (1 Cor. 12). Disunity affects the whole church, including its work of evangelism. In John 17, Jesus prayed for the unity of the church so the world would believe that God sent his Son to be Saviour of the world. Authentic church unity, which is a startling contrast to the strife of the world, is a sign to the world of the unity that exists between the Father and the Son.

Christians therefore should work for unity in the church. As John Murray wrote, 'If we are once convinced of the evil of schism in the body of Christ . . . we shall then be constrained to preach the evil, to bring conviction to the hearts of others also, to implore God's grace and wisdom in remedying the evil, and to devise ways and means of healing these ruptures' (*Collected Writings,* 2:335). We need to follow Matthew Henry's advice: 'In the great things of religion be of one mind, but when there is not a unity of sentiment, let there be a union of affections.'

Despite unbiblical splits, true believers will continue to be united as members of one body of Christ until the end of time, when every external division will disappear. There will be no divisions in heaven. In heaven, Christ's prayer that all believers may be one will find true fulfilment (John 17:20–26). The unity of the body of Christ will be resplendent (Rev. 7:9–17). What we now can hardly believe by faith will become gloriously evident by sight.

Chapter 13

Our Challenge as Citizens

Finally, our challenge to defeat Satan as Christian citizens in our respective nations involves resolutions that we should make in the strength of Christ by faith:

1. *Resolve to evangelise by spreading the truth wherever possible.* Satan is the father of liars; he is both liar and the lie. He is the antithesis of God, who is the essence of truth. God the Father declares truth (John 1:18), God the Son is the personification of truth (John 1:17; 14:6), and God the Holy Spirit leads us into truth (John 17:17; 16:13). God is absolute, unconditional truth; he cannot lie or be untruthful (Titus 1:2; Heb. 6:18). As Psalm 111:7–8 says, 'The works of his hands are truth and judgment; all his precepts are sure. They stand fast for ever and ever, and are done in truth and uprightness.' Truth is a glorious attribute of God. All lies are sin, for they are a contradiction of God as truth.

   God loves truth. Thomas Goodwin said, 'God hath but three things dear unto him in this world—his saints, his worship, and his truth, and it is hard to say which of these is dearest unto him.' People who are committed to Satan's downfall and Christ's increase are truth-spreaders. Resolve to be such a person.

   Do you ask, how do I go about that? Truth-spreading begins in the closet of prayer. Ask God every morning to make your life a force for truth that day. Ask him to help you forget yourself and remember him by proclaiming his truth in what you say and do. Pray for openings to speak a good word for God, then anticipate and act upon such opportunities. Force yourself not to let any opportunity slip by without saying some word for good. The more you do that, the easier it will become.

Let me give you two quick examples. As pastor of a large church, I am often asked to visit people in the hospital. When I get on the elevator, I usually make it a point to converse with those who are riding with me. I break the typical silence on elevators with a friendly comment or two, perhaps about the weather. Most of the time other people respond warmly. I then ask, 'Do you have a relative or a good friend in the hospital?' In almost every case, they do, so they talk about whom they are seeing and what the situation is. If we get off at the same floor, conversation often continues. I have had many opportunities to pray with such people, who, minutes before, had been total strangers to me. I have often followed up those pastoring opportunities by sending them Reformed literature.

I also initiate conversation with people on airplanes. I have resolved to do that whenever I fly alone. At first that was hard work, but over time, I have come to enjoy witnessing to people on airplanes. For one thing, due to the anonymity of airplanes, people are almost always willing to open up about their lives. Most of the time, they accept some Reformed literature that I purposely carry with me. Before we land, I offer to send them more free literature. About half of the people accept that offer and provide me with their address.

No doubt many of these efforts remain fruitless, but who can tell? Ecclesiastes 11:1 says, 'Cast thy bread upon the waters: for thou shalt find it after many days.' One time while flying over New York state, I gave some literature to a stewardess, who was an unbeliever. As we were landing, she asked me if I would send her some sermons by tape because she had to drive ninety miles to work every day. I sent her twenty tapes. A few weeks later, she sent me a letter expressing how much the sermons meant to her, and included a cheque of $50. Needless to say, I sent her more tapes.

Life is incredibly short. Let the truth convict you of sin, liberate you in Christ, and transform you into a spreader of truth. 'Keep the truth, and the truth will keep you', said William Bridge. Spread the truth wherever you can, in whatever way best fits the gifts that God has given you. Spread truth in private conversations, tracts, tapes, periodicals, books, radio, and email. Spread truth in your home, your church, your Sunday school, and among your neighbours. Spread truth in society, in jails, in nursing homes, and on the street.

A friend in Cape Town, South Africa gives himself to a full-time, faith ministry of spreading John Blanchard's *Ultimate Questions* to anyone who will receive them. He has numerous stories to tell of how God has blessed the handing out of tens of thousands of these booklets. His greatest expense is buying several pairs of shoes each year, due to their wearing out from his walking the streets for ten to twelve hours a day. Closer to home, I have an uncle in his eighties who always carries in his pocket several copies of the Inheritance Publishers' sermon booklets. Wherever he goes, he seeks to spread truth by striking up a conversation with people with the goal of getting a booklet into their hands. Once, at a church meeting, we heard numerous sirens; he disappeared for a while, only to return with great excitement. 'A large crowd had gathered around a motorcyclist who had hit a car, flipped onto the grass, and was doing well', he said. 'But, best of all', he added, opening his suit coat, and showing his empty pockets, 'I was able to give away all my sermons in one place!'

What truth do we spread? If we are not saved, we pervert truth and our lives spread lies, for we belong to the liar, Satan. Every moment that we do not glorify God, live by faith, and walk according to the spirit of the law, we bear false witness to our Creator. If we are saved, our lives must increasingly spread the truth, for we are of Christ, who is the Truth. Do not be shy about speaking up for Christ. The world isn't shy about its false agenda; why should Christians be shy about telling others about life-changing Truth? Thomas Brooks wrote, 'Every parcel of truth is precious as the filings of gold; we must either live with it, or die for it.'

If you would expose Satan's weakness, resolve to live as lights on the hill and salt in the earth. Let your life be contagious. Let love and truth abound, remembering that the deepest need of our nation is not the legislation of godliness and morality from the top down but the conversion of ordinary people, one at a time, from the grass roots level. One-on-one evangelism, not national politics, can save our backslidden countries.

Buy the truth (Prov. 23:23). Be a prayerful, persistent, dedicated spreader of truth. Know the truth (John 8:32), do the truth (John 3:21), and abide in the truth (John 8:44). Be a truth-teller and a truth-liver. Follow the advice of John Hus: 'Search the truth, hear truth, learn truth, love truth, speak the truth, hold the truth till death.' Then your salt will not lose its saltiness as a Christian citizen of your nation.

2. *Resolve to extend Christ's love to the poor and needy.* Satan's cause gets stronger when Christians turn a blind eye and deaf ear to social concerns. James sternly warns us of God's judgement on not caring for people in need. He says, 'If a brother or sister be naked, and destitute of daily food, and one of you say unto them, Depart in peace, be ye warmed and filled; notwithstanding ye give them not those things which are needful to the body; what doth it profit? Even so faith, if it hath not works, is dead, being alone' (2:15–17).

We must reach out to our needy neighbour both in word and deed. As John Stott said: 'Why should Christians get involved? In the end there are only two possible attitudes which Christians can adopt towards the world: Escape and Engagement.' 'Escape', Stott explains, means turning our backs on the world. It means rejecting unbelievers, washing our hands of them, and steeling our hearts against their agonised cries for help. By contrast, 'engagement' means turning our faces toward the world in compassion and getting our hands dirty, sore and worn in its service. It means, 'feeling deep within us the stirring of the love of which cannot be contained'. Stott concludes: 'If we truly love our neighbours, and ... desire to serve them, we shall be concerned for their total welfare, the well-being of their soul, their body and their community. And our concern will lead to practical programmes" (*Decisive Issues Facing Christians Today*, pp. 14, 19).

The Dutch Reformed liturgy for marriage challenges a new husband to work faithfully so that he may maintain his household honestly 'and likewise have something to give to the poor' (*Psalter,* p. 77). What are we giving of our time and financial resources to help the poor? Are we reaching out to them in word and deed?

3. *Resolve to speak out on scriptural and moral issues.* Many Christians avoid getting involved in politics because their efforts seem so ineffective. Yet, perhaps one reason that political life has degenerated is that God's people are often no longer getting involved.

    We need to seriously consider two things: first, God has established civil authorities to execute justice, to establish order and righteousness in society, and to provide for the common good. He does that to provide a peaceable context in which the gospel, godliness, and honesty may prosper (Rom. 13:1–7; Ps. 106:3; Isa. 1:17; 1 Tim. 2:1–2).

    Second, we have a responsibility to support our government. We must pay what we owe to the government (Mark 12:13–17) and pray for those in authority over us (1 Tim. 2:1–4). We must respect and obey the state, but our obedience to the state is not blind obedience. The apostles said that Christians should not obey civil authorities if their mandates contradict God's laws (Acts 5:29). Paul used his Roman citizenship to object to injustice (Acts 16:35–39; 22:24–29). Other biblical characters influenced the secular government that ruled over them. Consider the examples of Joseph (Gen. 41) and Daniel (Dan. 6).

We should carefully consider whom to vote for in local and national elections. As John Jay, the first chief justice of the United States Supreme Court, said in 1816: 'Providence has given to our people the choice of their rulers, and it is the duty ... of our Christian nation to select and prefer Christians for their rulers' (*Correspondence and Public Papers of John Jay* [New York: G.P. Putnam, 1893], 4:393).

Christians are to be salt and light in the world and that world includes the government. J. I. Packer writes, 'The more profoundly one is concerned about heaven, the more deeply one cares about God's will being done on earth.'

How far should a Christian go in supporting state and political affairs? Here are four principles to guide us:

a. *Study Scripture for guidance*. Understand what the Bible has to say on moral issues like abortion, euthanasia, homosexuality, and Sabbath desecration. Read appropriate materials that will give you a working vocabulary and knowledge of these issues, and then speak to your family, friends, work associates, and neighbours about them.

b. *Pray daily for civil authorities*. Pray for the conversion of those who are unsaved and for the strengthening of those who are Christians (1 Tim. 2:1–2). Pray for revival in the land. Cry to God, 'Save thy people, and bless thine inheritance. Turn us again, O LORD God of hosts, cause thy face to shine; and we shall be saved' (Ps. 28:9; 80:19). Could one reason why we see so little of God's movement in society be related to our shallow prayers, our minimal expectation of God, and our neglect to view ourselves as personally involved in the sins of our land? When King Edward died suddenly in England, John Bradford confessed, 'He died because of my sin.' Bradford, as a Christian citizen, viewed himself as part of the corporate nation, and thus confessed guilt for his lack of prayer for his God-fearing king. This inclusion of ourselves in prayer for the nation is biblical—for example, notice how Daniel includes himself repeatedly in confessing corporate, national guilt in his well-known prayer in Daniel 9.

c. *Learn how your government operates.* Political institutions are imperfect in this fallen world, but remember that God has ordained them. Governments legislate morality. The question is whose morality will be legislated. If Christians ignore what is happening in government and put their head in the sand, their country will deteriorate even faster.

Note, however, that the church is not to be a political institution. The church helps to bring people to Christ and then moulds them to be like him. Believers who are motivated by Christ's love and compassion then may enter the political arena well-equipped to stand firm for justice.

d. *Get involved.* Write letters to government leaders and editors of newspapers and other media that influence political processes. Join organisations and support movements that uphold Christian morality. Run for public office, if God calls you to do that. Otherwise, support other Christians who sustain biblical views and do run for office.

Finally, when you contemplate raising your voice on moral issues of the day, remember Luther's famous statement: 'If I profess with the loudest voice and the clearest exposition every portion of the truth of God, except precisely that little point which the world and the devil are at that moment attacking, I am not confessing Christ, however boldly I may be professing Christ. Where the battles rages, there the loyalty of the soldier is proved.'

Live for Christ

Paul wrote to the Ephesians, 'Neither give place to the devil' (4:27). Leave no opening for the devil. Be too busy for Satan. Do not allow empty spaces in your life, for the devil will surely fill them. Do not serve Satan, who is a squatter without rights in this world. As a believer, you have no business sinning or living like an unbeliever. By God's grace, mortify all lust, bitterness, and anger. Live for Christ.

'Who is sufficient for these things?' 2 Cor. 2:16 asks. For years I thought that was a rhetorical question to be answered with, 'Certainly not me and no one else, either.' But Paul answers the question six verses later: 'Not that we are sufficient of ourselves to think any thing as of ourselves; but our sufficiency is of God' (2 Cor. 3:5). In the power of Christ, we can live a life to God's glory that triumphs over Satan's defeat—personally, in the church, and in the nation. Live for your Saviour who holds the world, the nations, the church, and yourself—including the smallest detail—in his almighty, gracious hands.

Let me close with a prayer of John Calvin: 'Grant, Almighty God, that as thou art graciously pleased daily to set before us thy sure and certain will, we may open our eyes and ears, and raise all our thoughts to that which not only reveals to us what is right, but also confirms us in a sound mind, so that we may go on in the course of true religion, and never turn aside, whatever Satan and his demons may devise against us, but that we may stand firm and persevere, until having finished our warfare, we shall at length come unto that blessed rest which has been prepared for us in heaven by Jesus Christ our Lord, Amen.'

Selected Bibliography

Alexander, William Menzies. *Demonic Possession in the New Testament: Its Historical, Medical, and Theological Aspects.* Grand Rapids: Baker, 1980.

Barnhouse, Donald Grey. *The Invisible War.* Grand Rapids: Zondervan, 1965.

Baskin, Wade. *Dictionary of Satanism.* New York: Philosophical Library, n.d.

Blades, Keith R. *Satan and His Plan of Evil: A Survey of the Biblical Doctrine.* Calgary: North Calgary Open Bible Fellowship, 1994.

Bounds, E. M. *Satan: His Personality, Power and Overthrow.* Grand Rapids: Baker, 1972.

Boyd, Gregory A. *God at War: The Bible and Spiritual Conflict.* Downners Grove, Ill.: InterVarsity Press, 1997.

Brooks, Thomas. *Precious Remedies Against Satan's Devices.* Edinburgh: Banner of Truth Trust, 1968.

Bufford, Rodger K. *Counseling and the Demonic.* Dallas: Word, 1988.

DeVries, Brian. 'Spiritual Wickedness in High Places: Biblical Demonology and the Church's Mission.' Unpublished paper for Introduction to Missions class, Puritan Reformed Theological Seminary, 2003.

Dickason, C. Fred. *Angels: Elect and Evil.* Chicago: Moody, 1975.

_____. *Demon Possession & the Christian.* Chicago: Moody, 1987.

Downame, John. *The Christian Warfare,* 2 vols. London: Felix Kyngston, 1609-1611.

Evans, Tony. *The Battle is the Lord's: Waging Victorious Spiritual*

Warfare. Chicago: Moody, 1998.

Feinberg, John S. *The Many Faces of Evil: Theological Systems and the Problems of Evil*. Wheaton, Ill.: Crossway, 2004.

Frederickson, Bruce G. *How to Respond [to] Satanism*. St. Louis: CPH, 1995.

Gilpin, Richard. *A Treatise on Satan's Temptations*. Morgan, Penn.: Soli Deo Gloria, 2000.

Goodwin, Thomas. "The Child of Light Walking in Darkness." *The Works of Thomas Goodwin*. Eureka, Calif.: Tanski Publications, 3:231-352.

Green, Michael. *I Believe in Satan's Downfall*. Grand Rapids: Eerdmans, 1981.

Gross, Edward N. *Miracles, Demons, and Spiritual Warfare: An Urgent call for Discernment*. Grand Rapids: Baker, 1991.

Gurnall, William. *The Christian in Complete Armour*. 3 vols (abridged). Edinburgh: Banner of Truth, 1986.

Jones, Peter. *The Gnostic Empire Strikes Back*. Phillipsburg: P&R, 1992.

Jones, Peter. *Spirit Wars: Pagan Revival in Christian America*. Mukilteo, WA: Wine Press Publishing, 1997.

Koch, Kurt E. *Satan's Devices*. Grand Rapids: Kregel, 1978.

Larson, Bob. *Satanism: The Seduction of America's Youth*. Nashville: Nelson, 1989.

Leahy, Frederick. *Satan Cast Out: A Study in Biblical Demonology*. Edinburgh: Banner of Truth, 1975.

_____. *The Victory of the Lamb: Christ's Triumph over Sin, Death and Satan*. Edinburgh: Banner of Truth Trust, 2001.

Lewis, C. S. *The Screwtape Letters*. New York: The Macmillan Company, 1944.

Lutzer, Erwin W. *The Serpent of Paradise: The Incredible Story of How Satan's Rebellion Serves God's Purposes*. Chicago: Moody, 1996.

MacArthur, John, Jr. *God, Satan, and Angels*. Panorama City, Calif.: Word of Grace Communications, 1983.

_____. *How to Meet the Enemy*. Wheaton, Ill.: Victor, 1992.

Matson, William A. *The Adversary, His Person, Power, and*

Purpose: A Study in Satanology. New York: Wilbur B. Ketcham, 1891.

Mayhue, Richard. *Unmasking Satan: Understanding Satan's Battle Plan and Biblical Strategies for Fighting Back.* Grand Rapids: Kregel's, 1998.

Miller, Andrew. *Meditations on the Christian's Standing, State, Vocation, Warfare and Hope.* London: G. Morrish.

Parsons, Wm. L. *Satan's Devices and the Believer's Victory.* Boston: Parsons, 1864.

Penn-Lewis, Jessie and Roberts, Evan. *War on the Saints.* Fort Washington, Penn.: The Christian Literature Crusade.

Phillips, John. *Exploring Genesis: An Expository Commentary.* Grand Rapids: Kregel, 2001.

Pink, A. W. *The Antichrist.* Grand Rapids: Kregel, 1988.

Pink, A. W. *Satan and His Gospel.* Swengel, PA: Reiner Publications, n.d.

Powlison, David. *Power Encounters: Reclaiming Spiritual Warfare.* Grand Rapids: Baker, 1995.

Prime, Derek. *Spiritual Warfare.* Springdale, PA: Whitaker House, 1987.

Russell, Jeffrey Burton. *Satan: the Early Christian Tradition.* Ithaca: Cornell University Press, 1981.

Spurgeon, Charles. *Satan a Defeated Foe.* Springdale, PA: Whitaker House, 1993.

Spurgeon, Charles. *Spurgeon on Prayer and Spiritual Warfare.* New Kensington, PA: Whitaker House, 1998.

Spurstowe, William. *The Wiles of Satan.* Morgan, Penn.: Soli Deo Gloria, 2004.

Townsend, L. T. *Satan and Demons.* New York: Eaton & Mains, 1902.

Unger, Merrill. *Biblical Demonology.* Wheaton, Ill.: Scripture Press, 1972.

_____. *What Demons Can Do To Saints.* Chicago: Moody, 1977.

Wagner, Peter, ed. *Territorial Spirits: Insights on Strategic-Level Spiritual Warfare from Nineteen Christian Leaders.*

Chichester, Eng.: Sovereign World, 1991.

Wiersbe, Warren W. *The Strategy of Satan: How to Detect and Defeat Him.* Wheaton: Tyndale, 1979.

Zacharias, Bryan. *The Embattled Christian: William Gurnall and the Puritan View of Spiritual Warfare.* Edinburgh: Banner of Truth Trust, 1995.